West Virginia Penitentiary
Coloring Book

C.J. Plogger

ISBN: 1717139477
ISBN-13: 978-1717139474

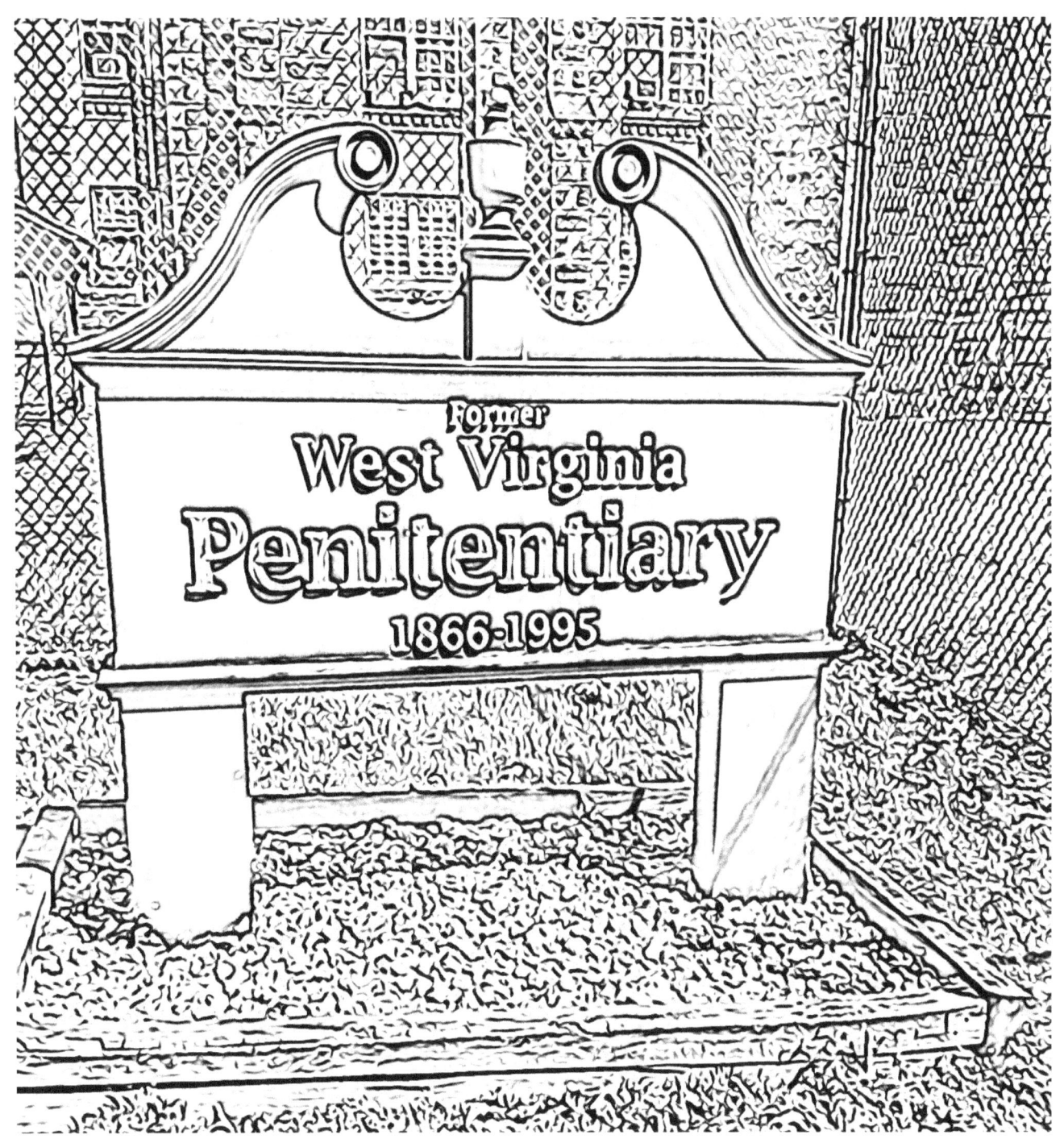

WELCOME TO THE WEST VIRGINIA PENITENTIARY!

We are glad that you came to see us.

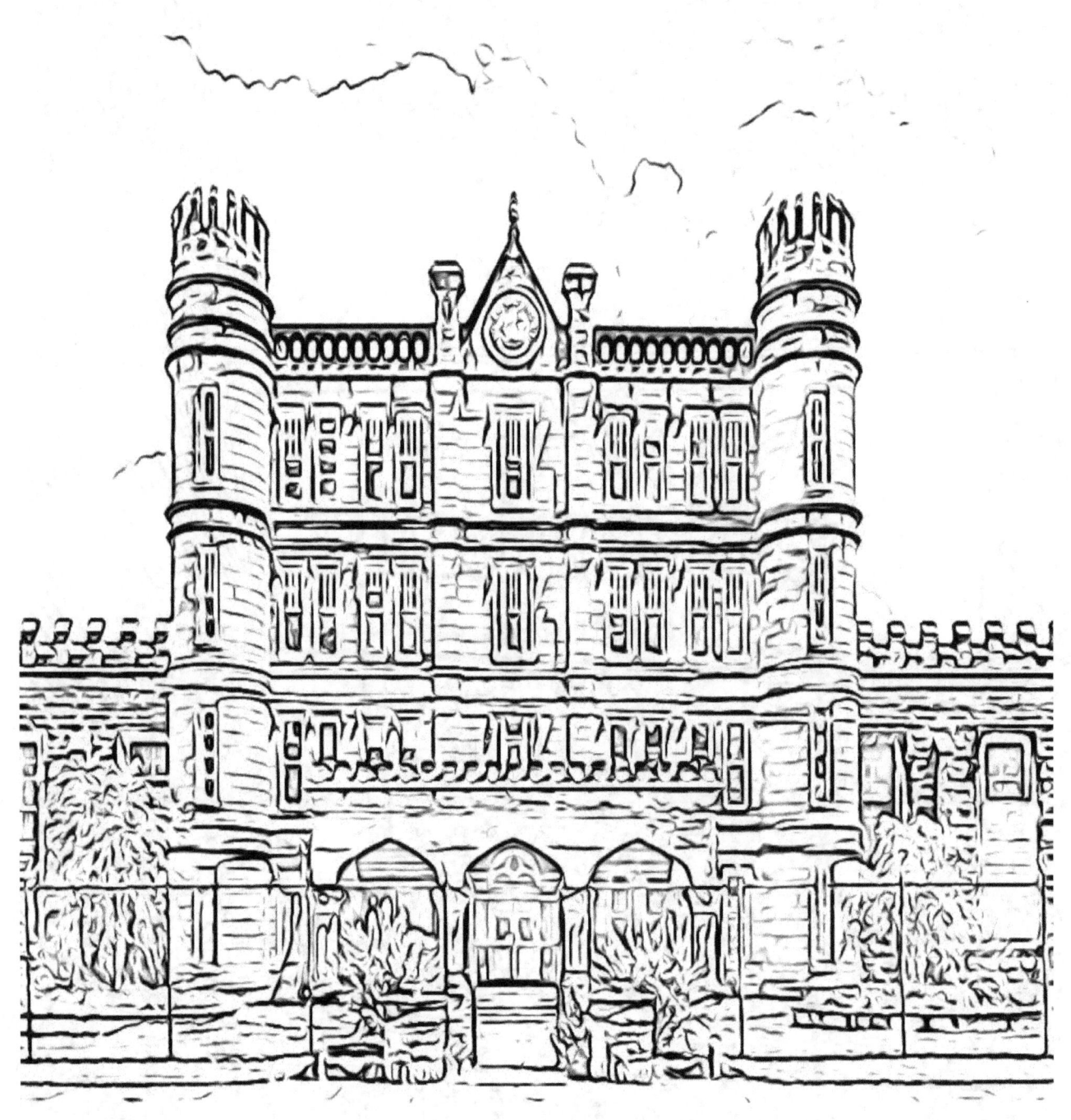

West Virginia Penitentiary

West Virginia Penitentiary started in 1866. It was closed on
March 27, 1995.

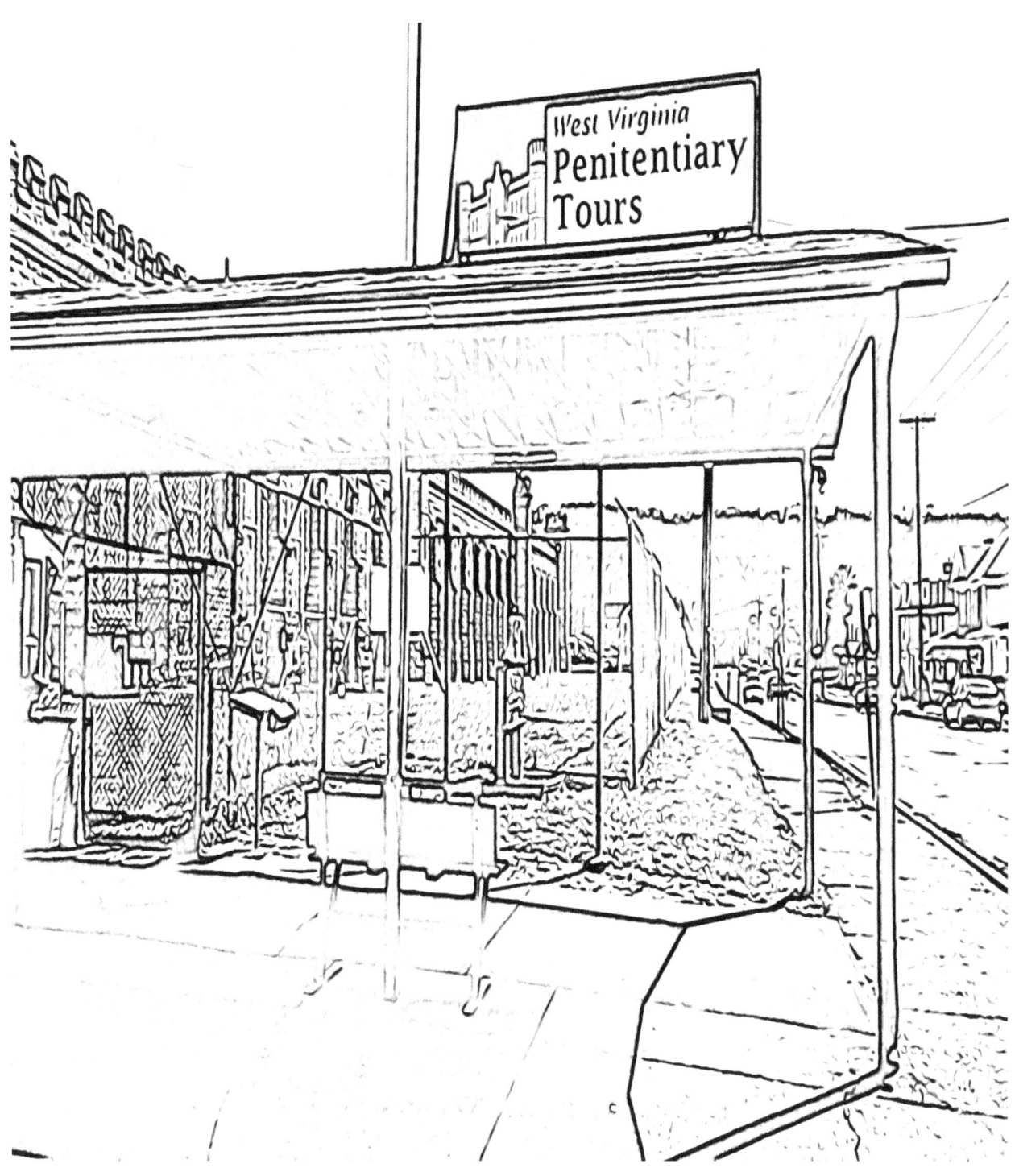

West Virginia Penitentiary

Come on in and take a tour!

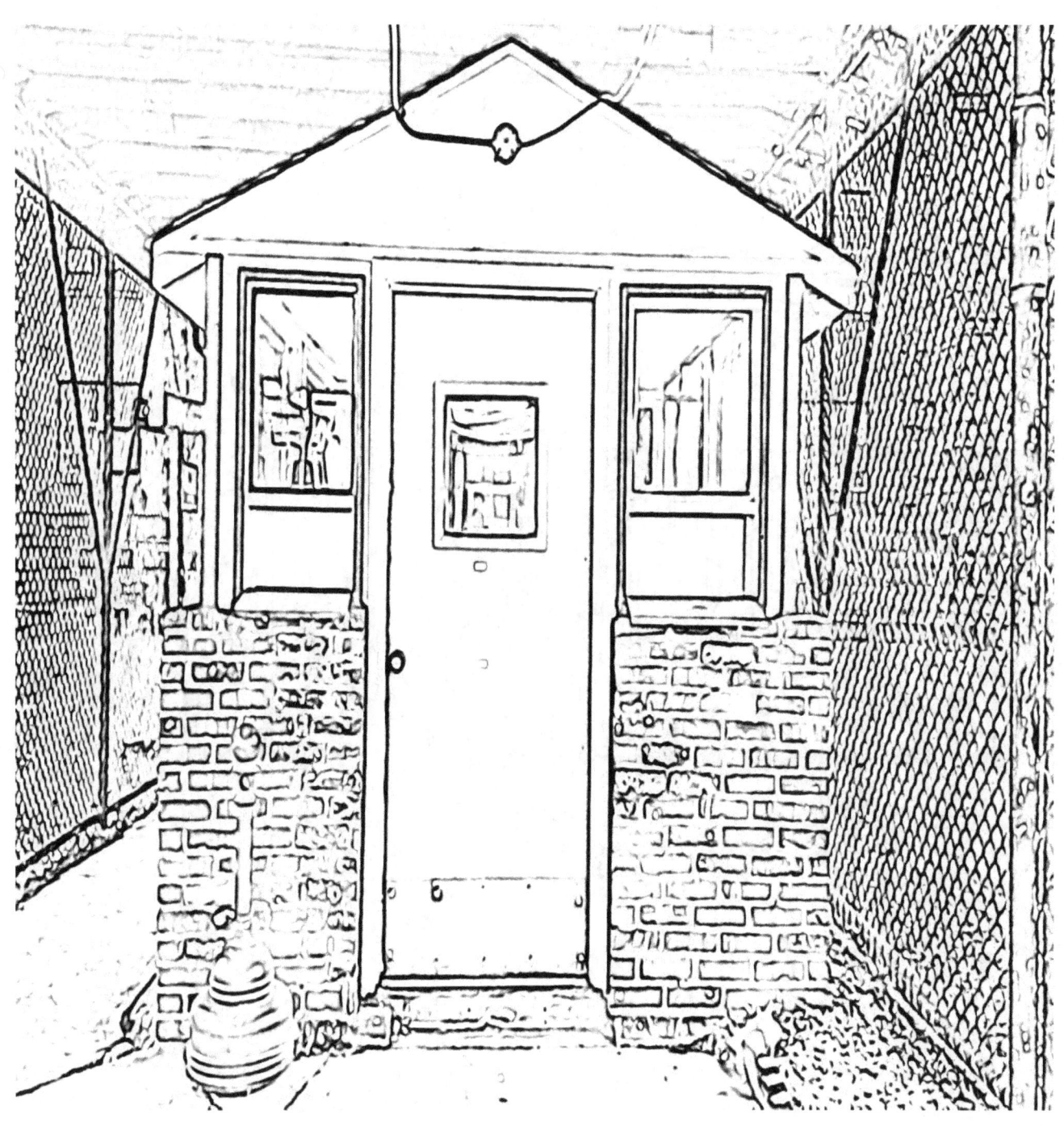

West Virginia Penitentiary

This is Post Pappa. This is where people came in and out of the penitentiary after 1959.

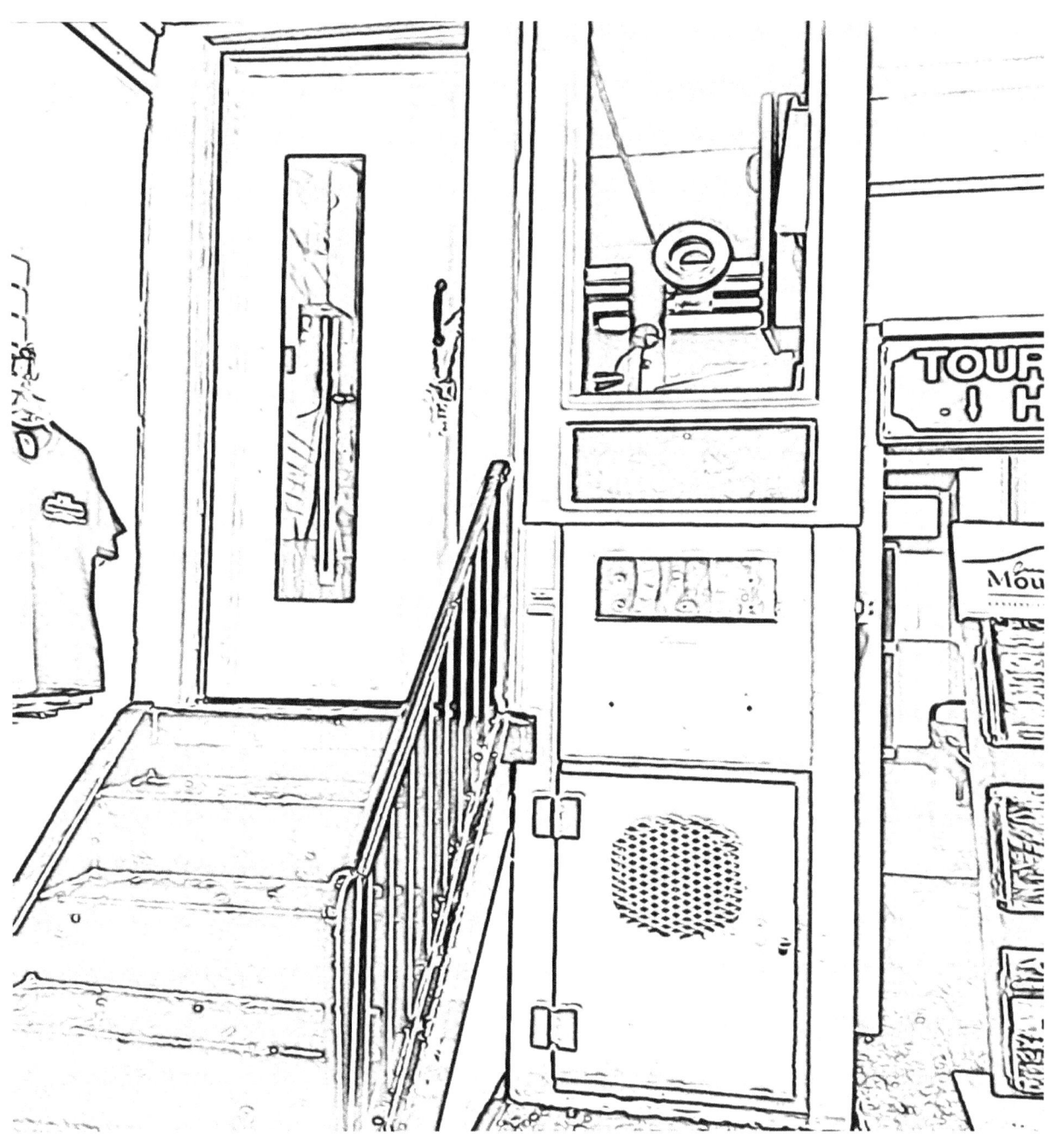

West Virginia Penitentiary

This is the Control Cage. The Correctional Officer would open the doors to let people in and out.

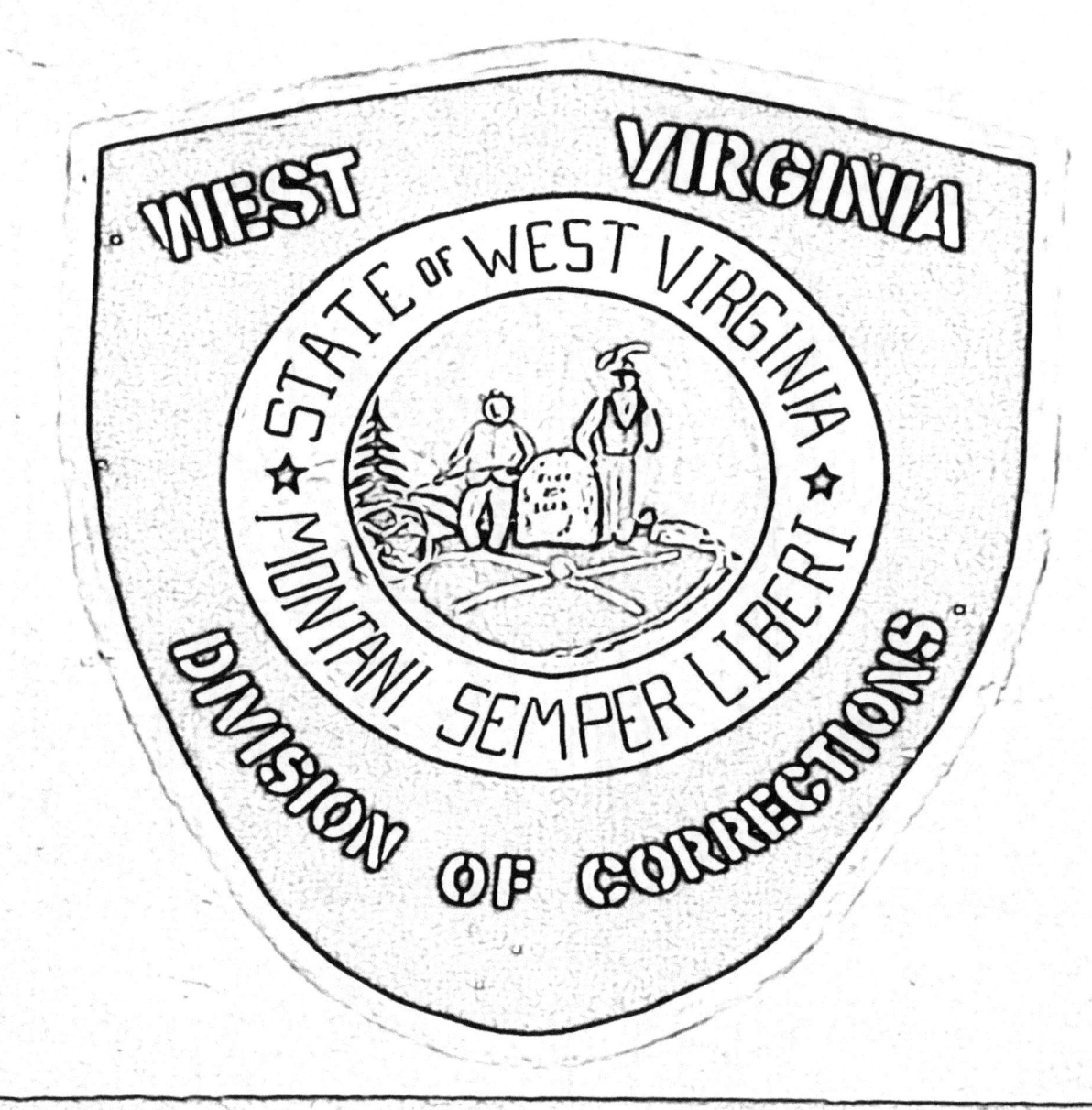

West Virginia Penitentiary

This is the badge for the West Virginia Division of Corrections. It is also the State Motto for West Virginia. You will pass it as you walk to the Non-Contact Visitation Room.

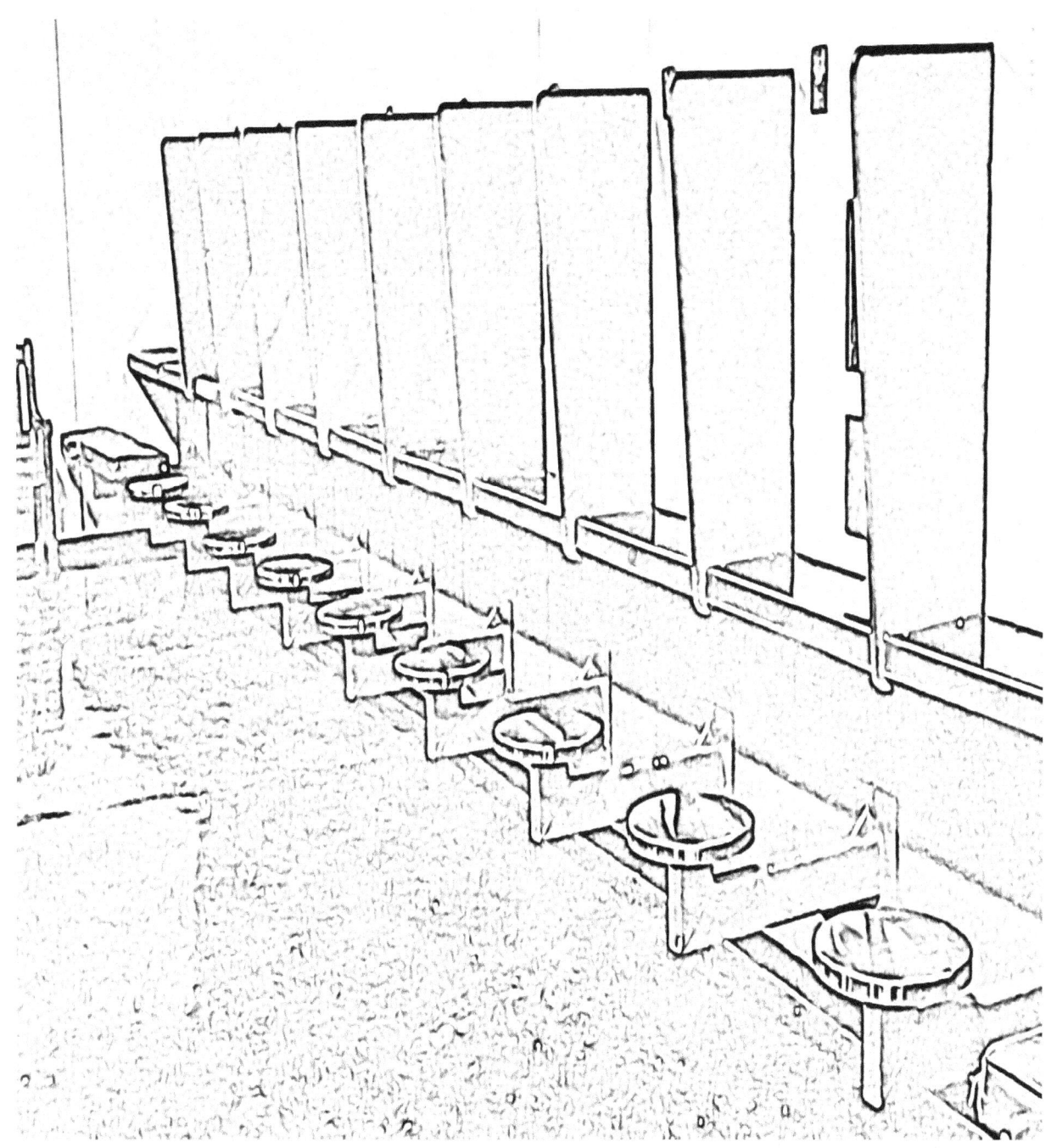

West Virginia Penitentiary

This is the Non-Contact Visitation Room. Family and friends would sit around the outside. The inmates sat on the seats and looked through the plexiglass.

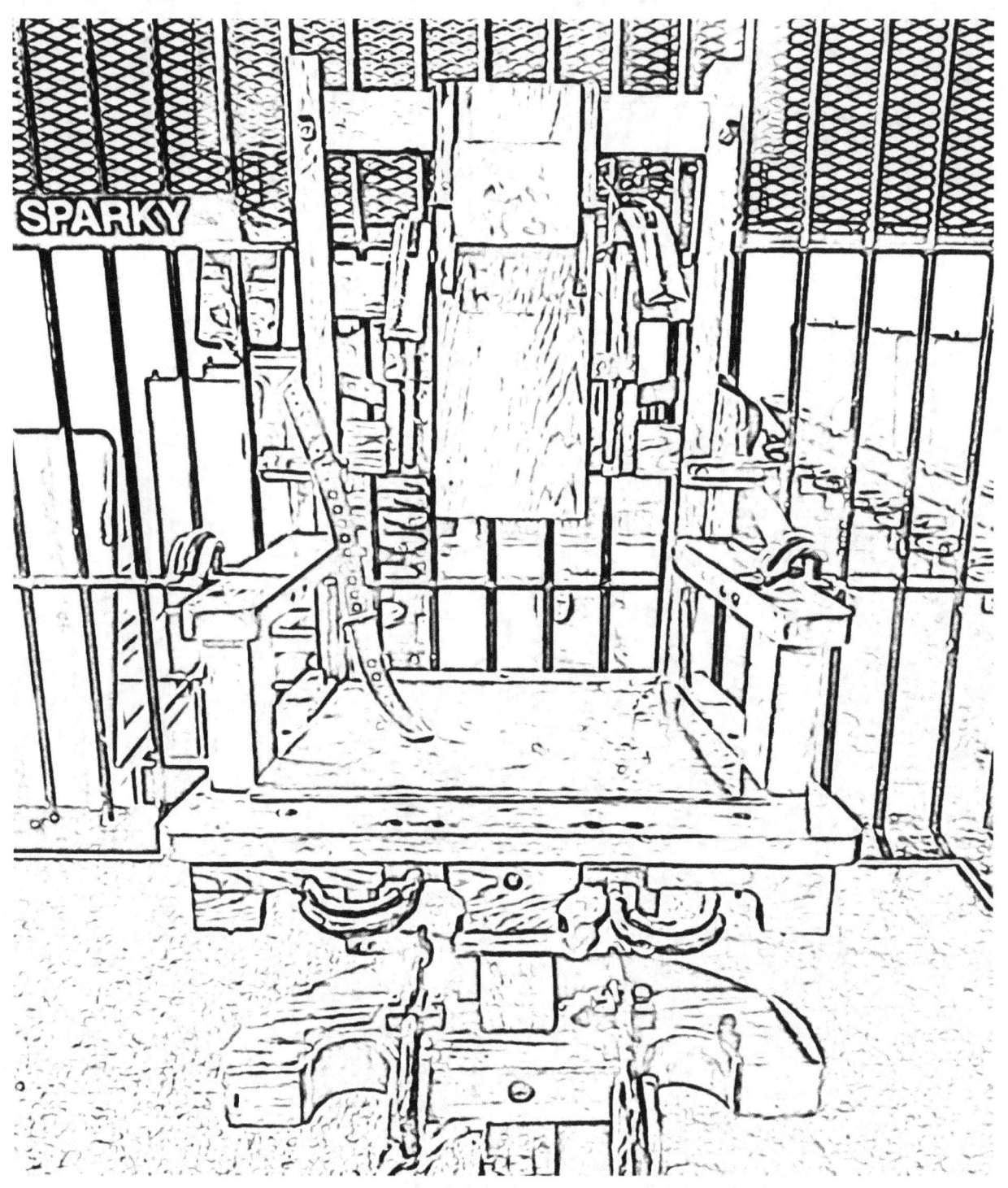

West Virginia Penitentiary

This is "Old Sparky". Nine men were executed on it.

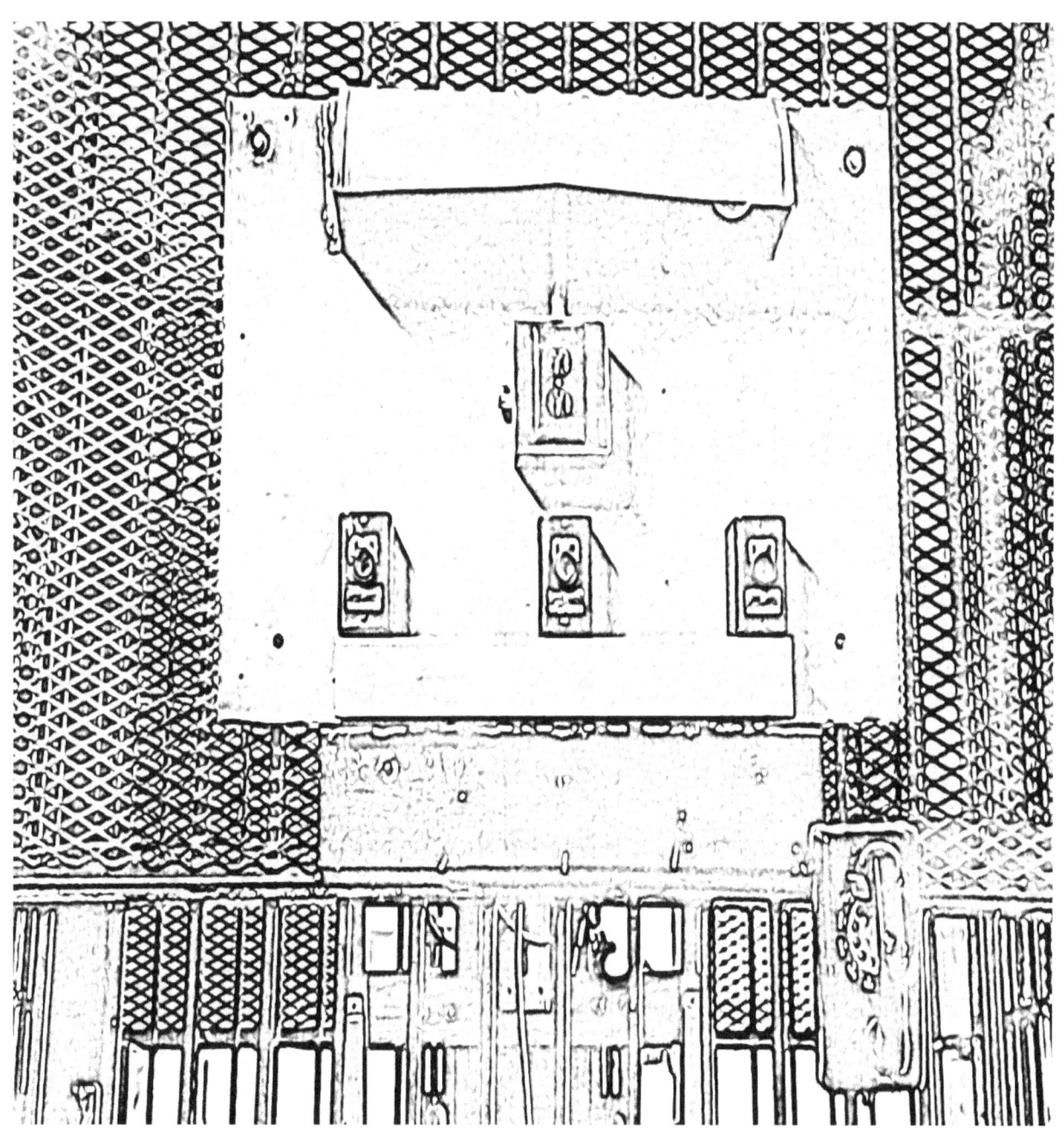

West Virginia Penitentiary

These were the buttons to send electricity to "Old Sparky". The phone on the right received calls from the Governor's office when he wanted to pardon someone.

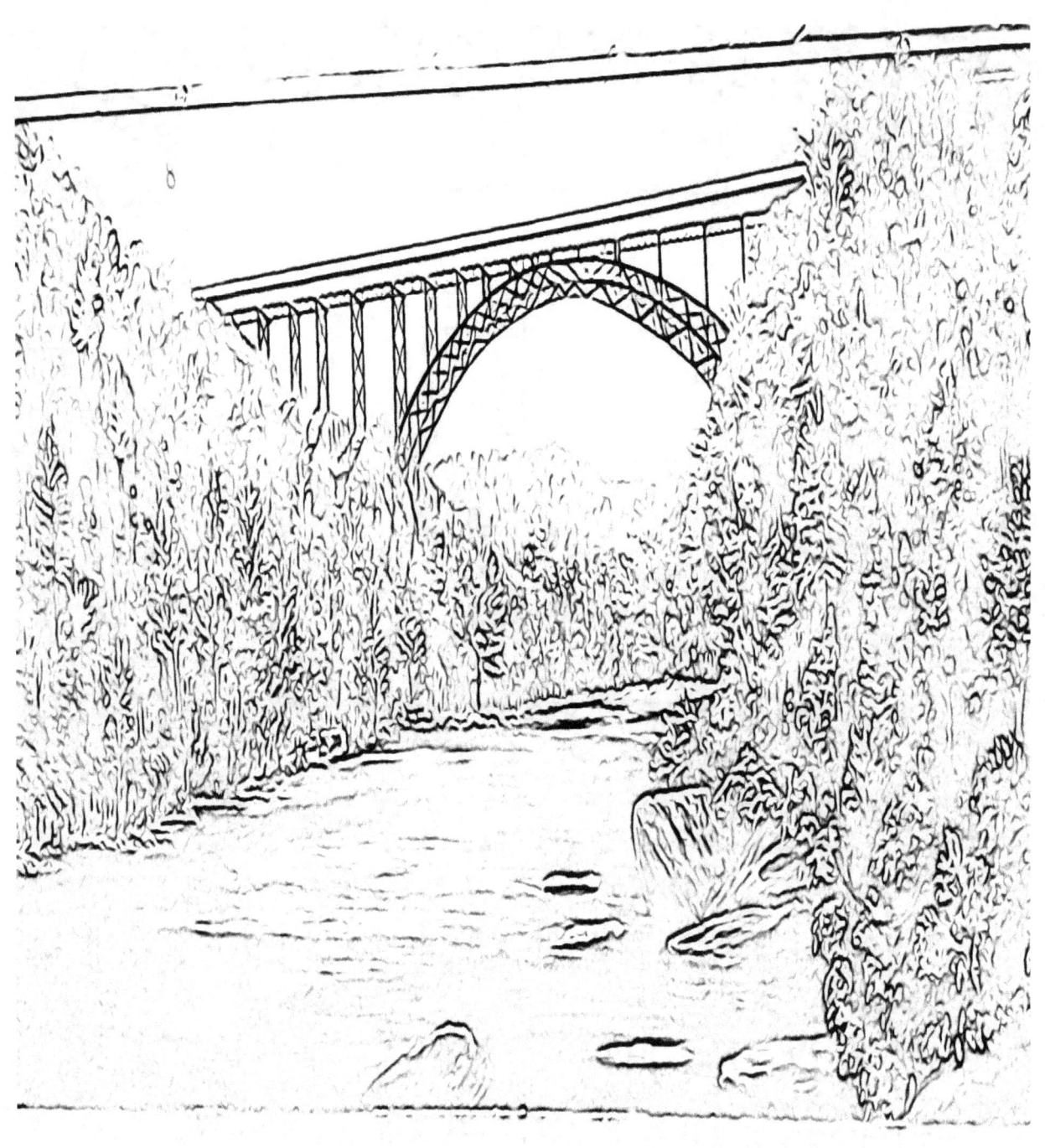

West Virginia Penitentiary

This painting is on the left wall when you leave the Non-Contact Visitation Room. It was painted by inmate, Danny Lehman.

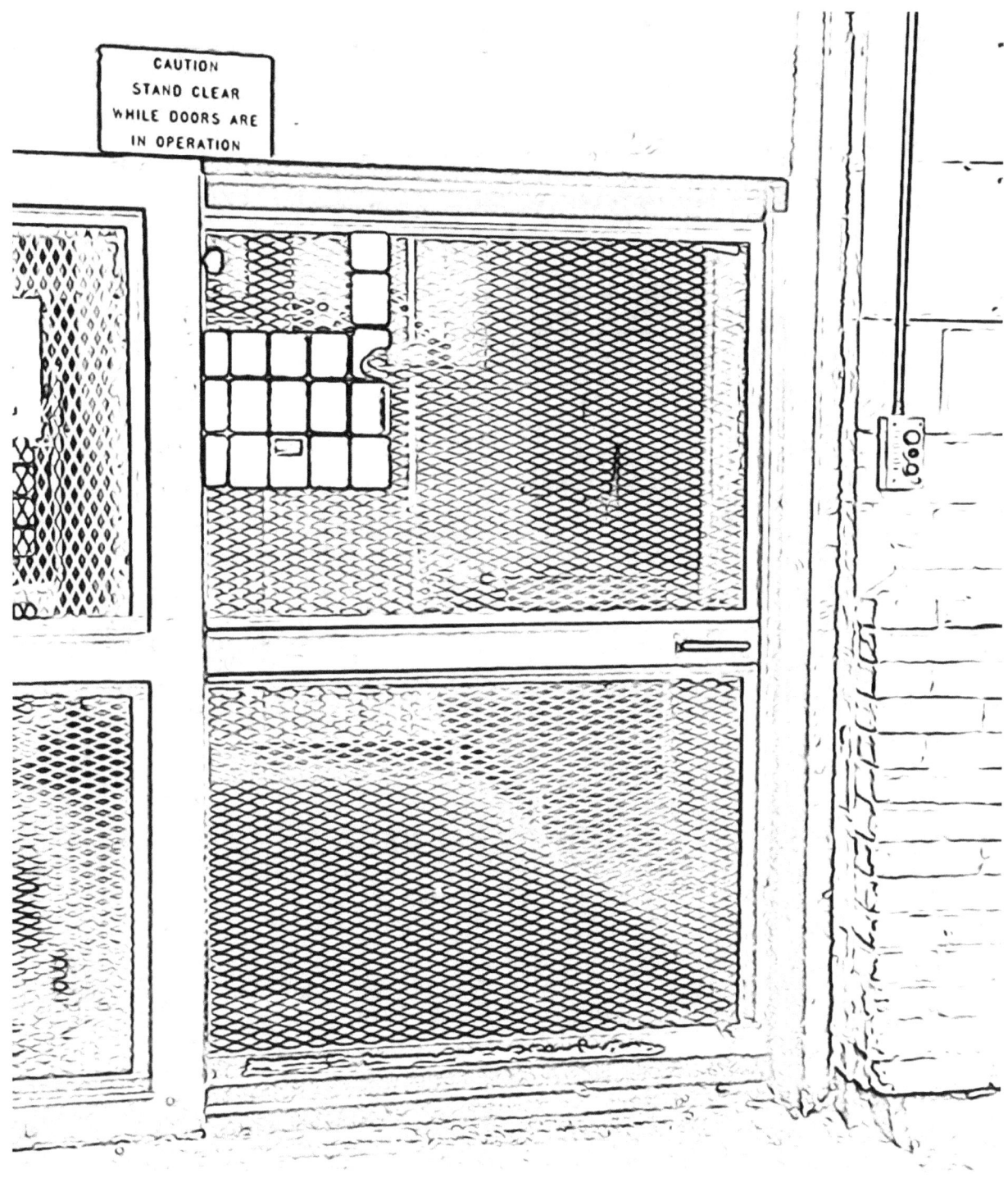

West Virginia Penitentiary

This is Door 5. It opens into the penitentiary on the 98 Corridor.

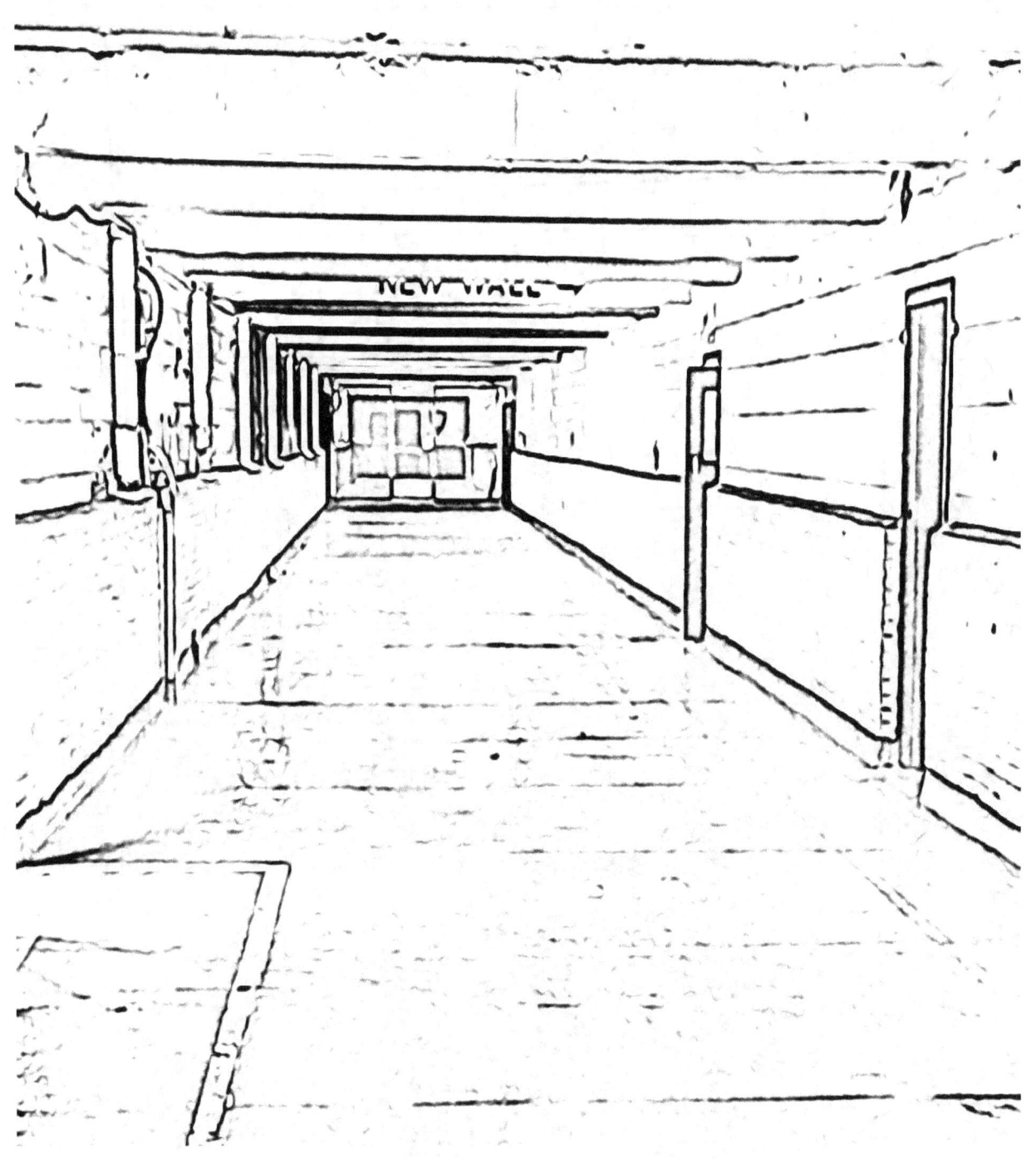

West Virginia Penitentiary

This is the 98 Corridor. This was the main hallway where many inmates went back and forth.

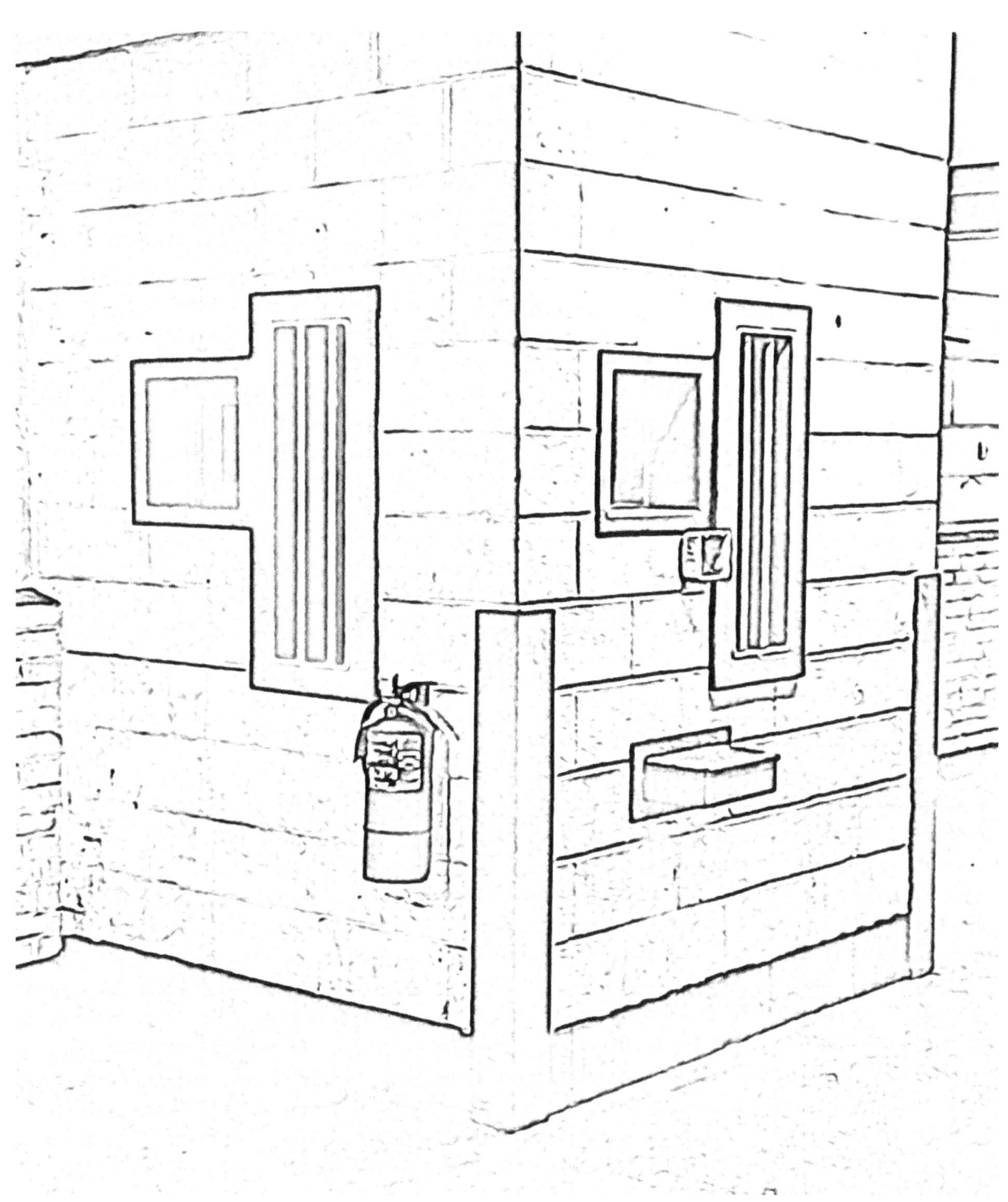

West Virginia Penitentiary

This is the Gun Cage on the 98 Corridor.

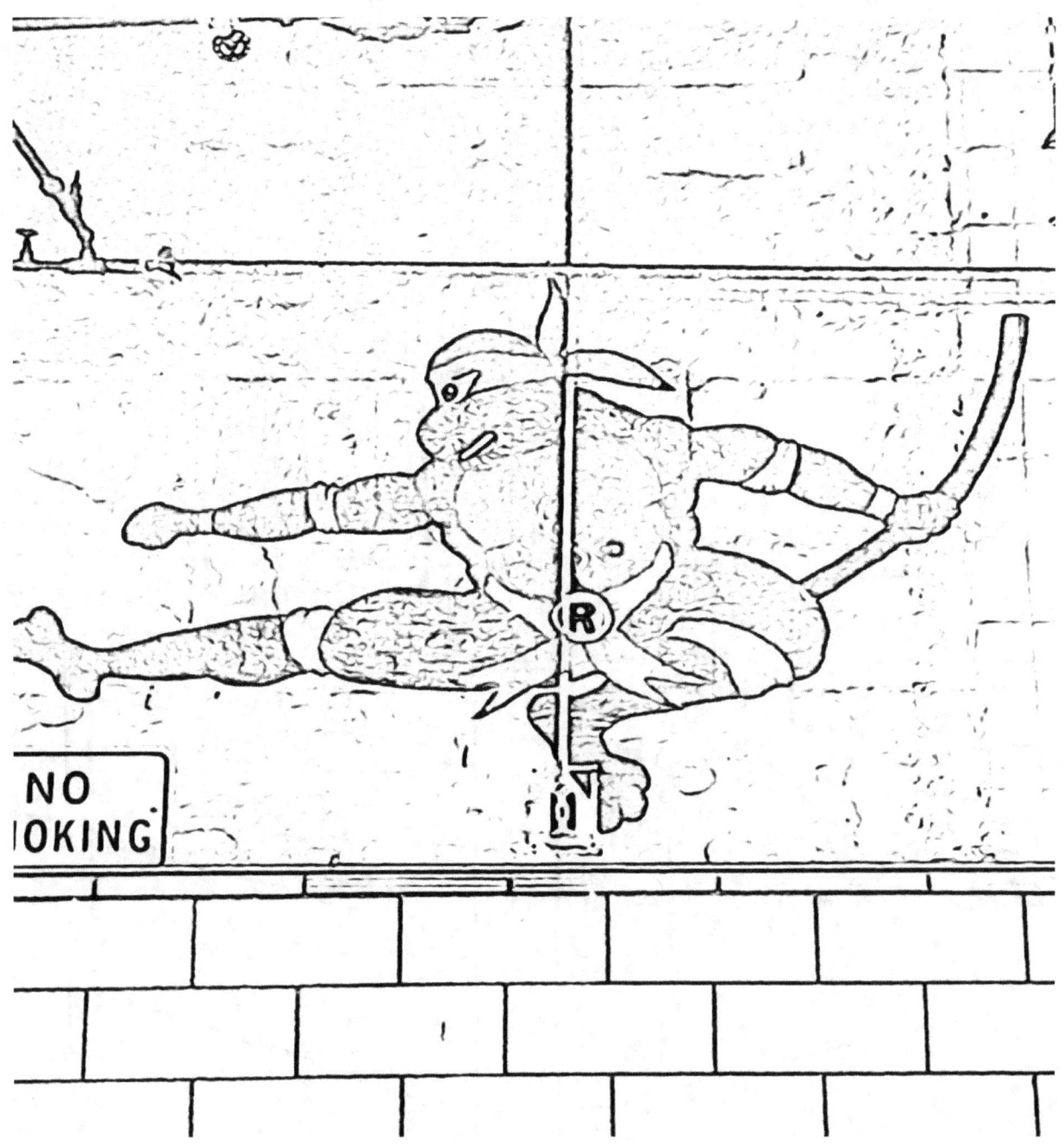

West Virginia Penitentiary

This area was the site of the first cells. Then it becomes the Dining Hall. After the 1986 riot, it becomes the Contact Visitation Room. Inmates painted these murals.

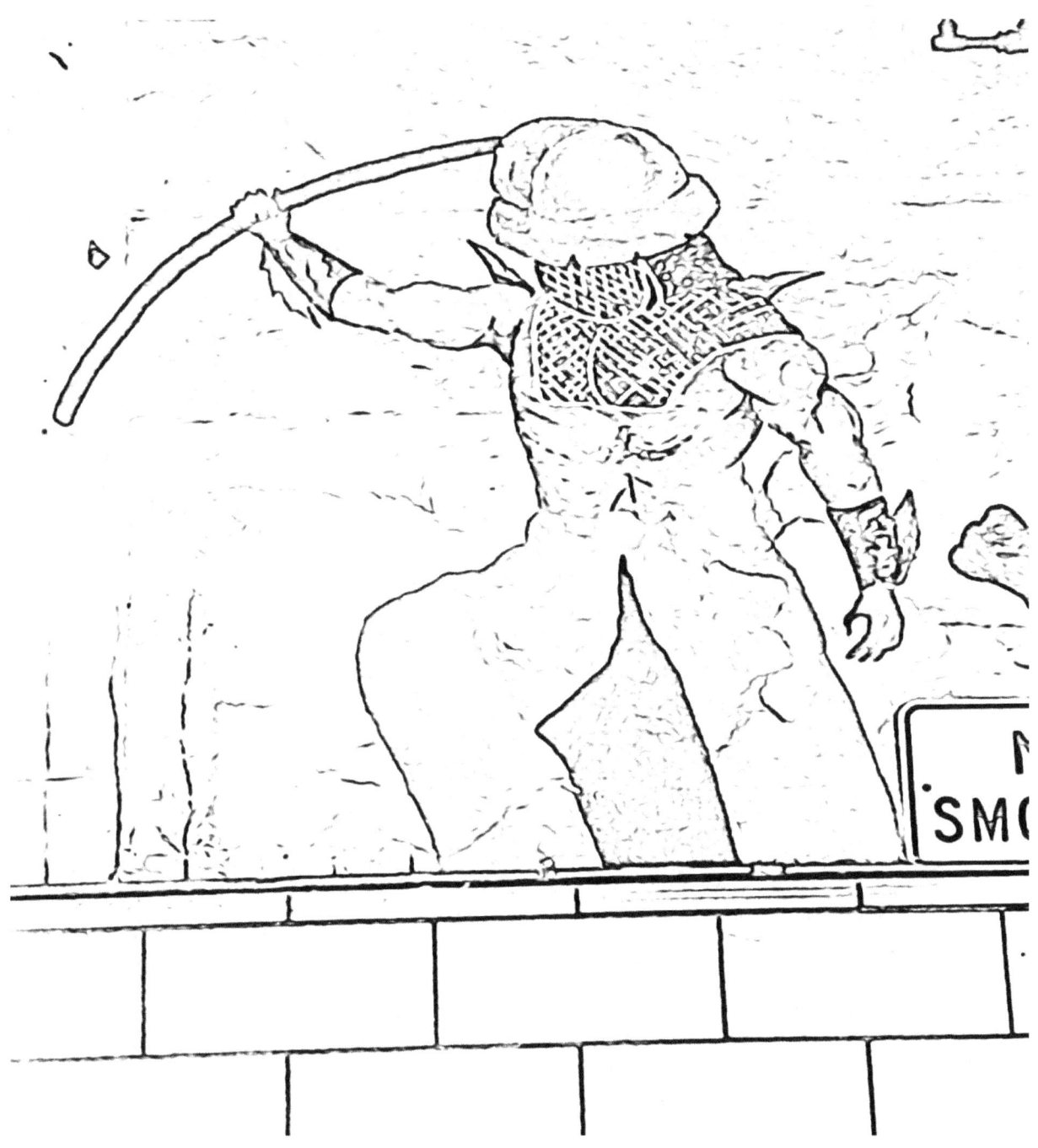

West Virginia Penitentiary

This mural is "Shredder", the enemy of the Teenage Mutant Ninja Turtles.

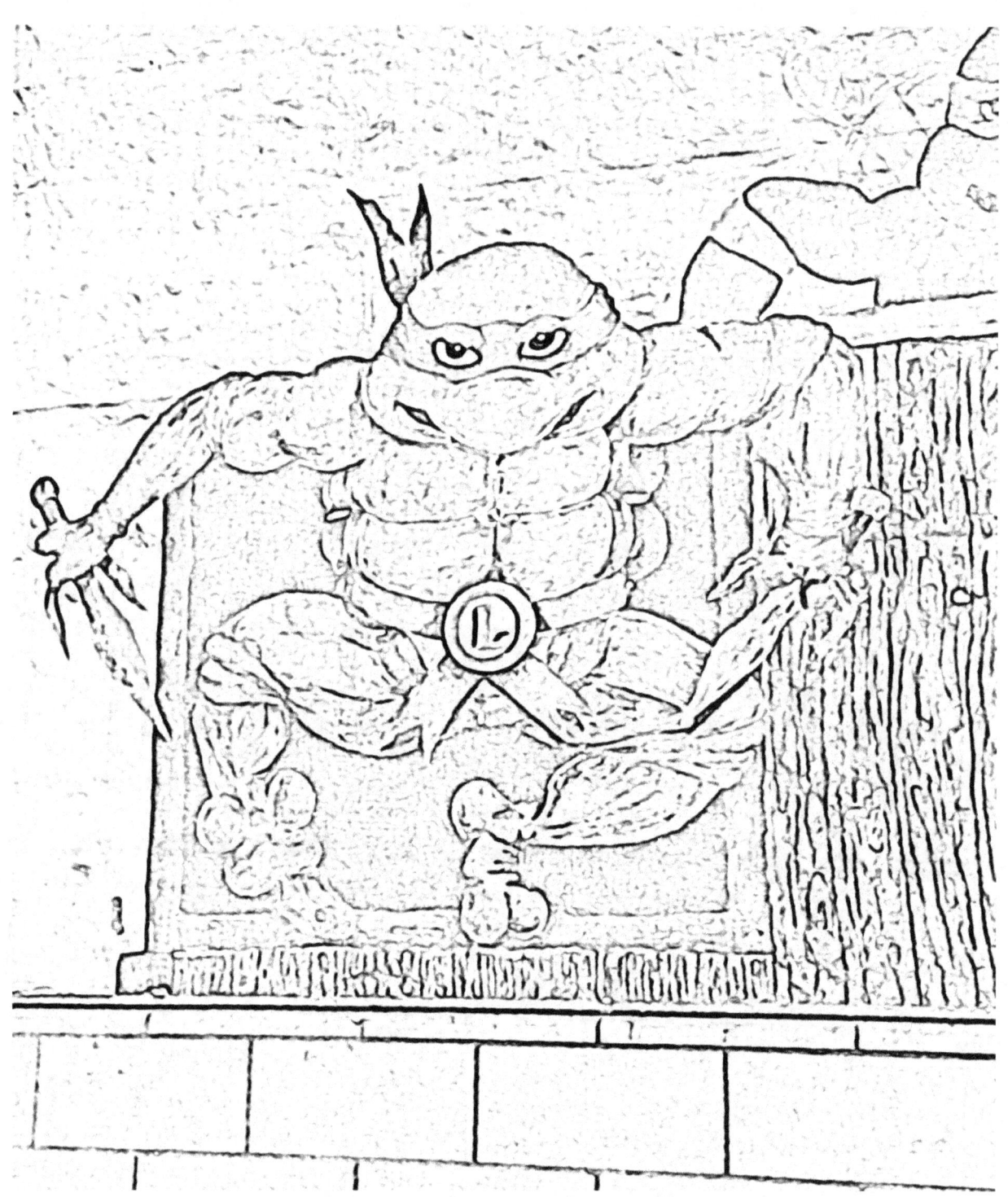

West Virginia Penitentiary

This mural is another one of the Teenage Mutant Ninja Turtles.

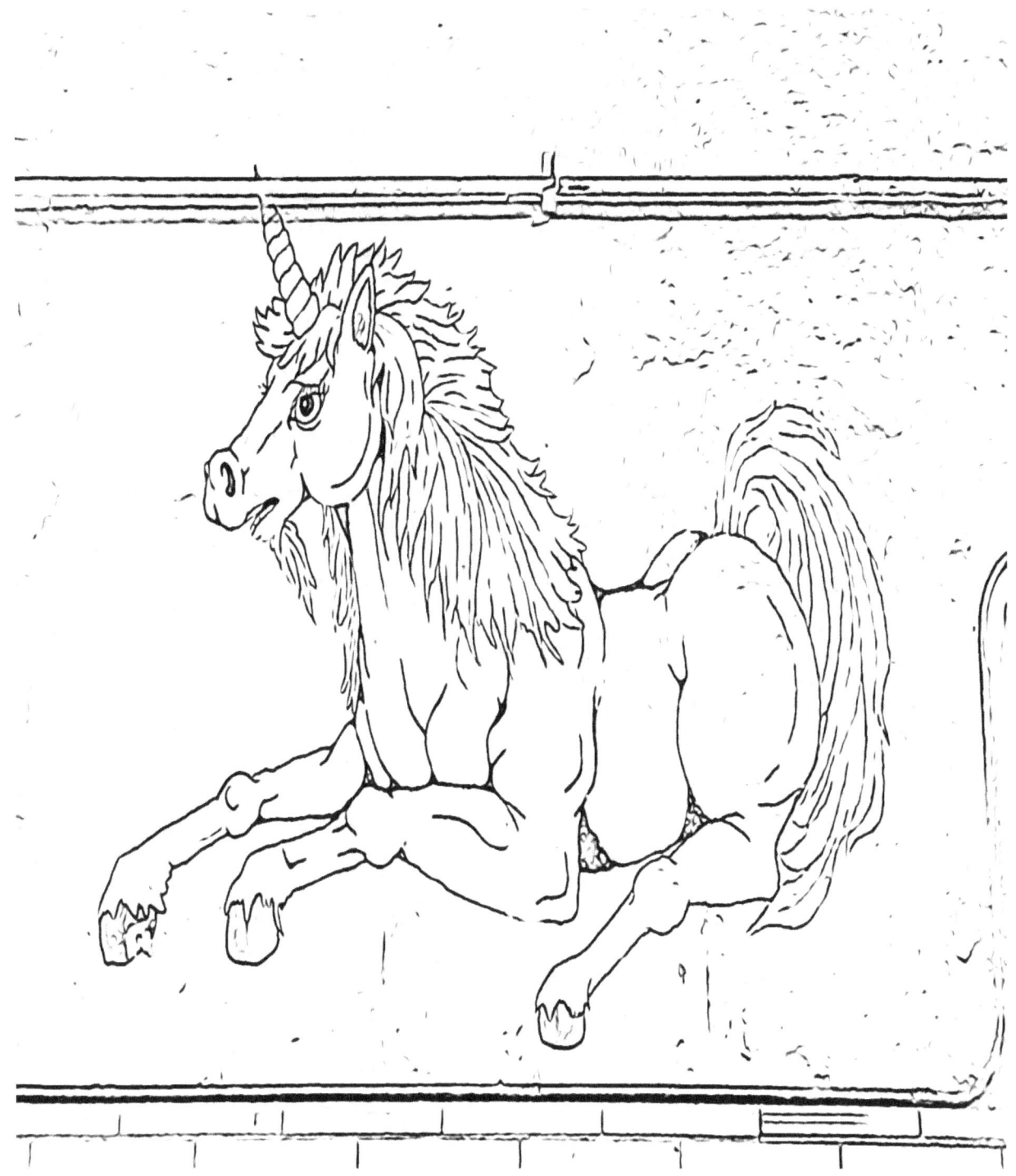

West Virginia Penitentiary

This mural in the Contact Visitation Room is a unicorn.

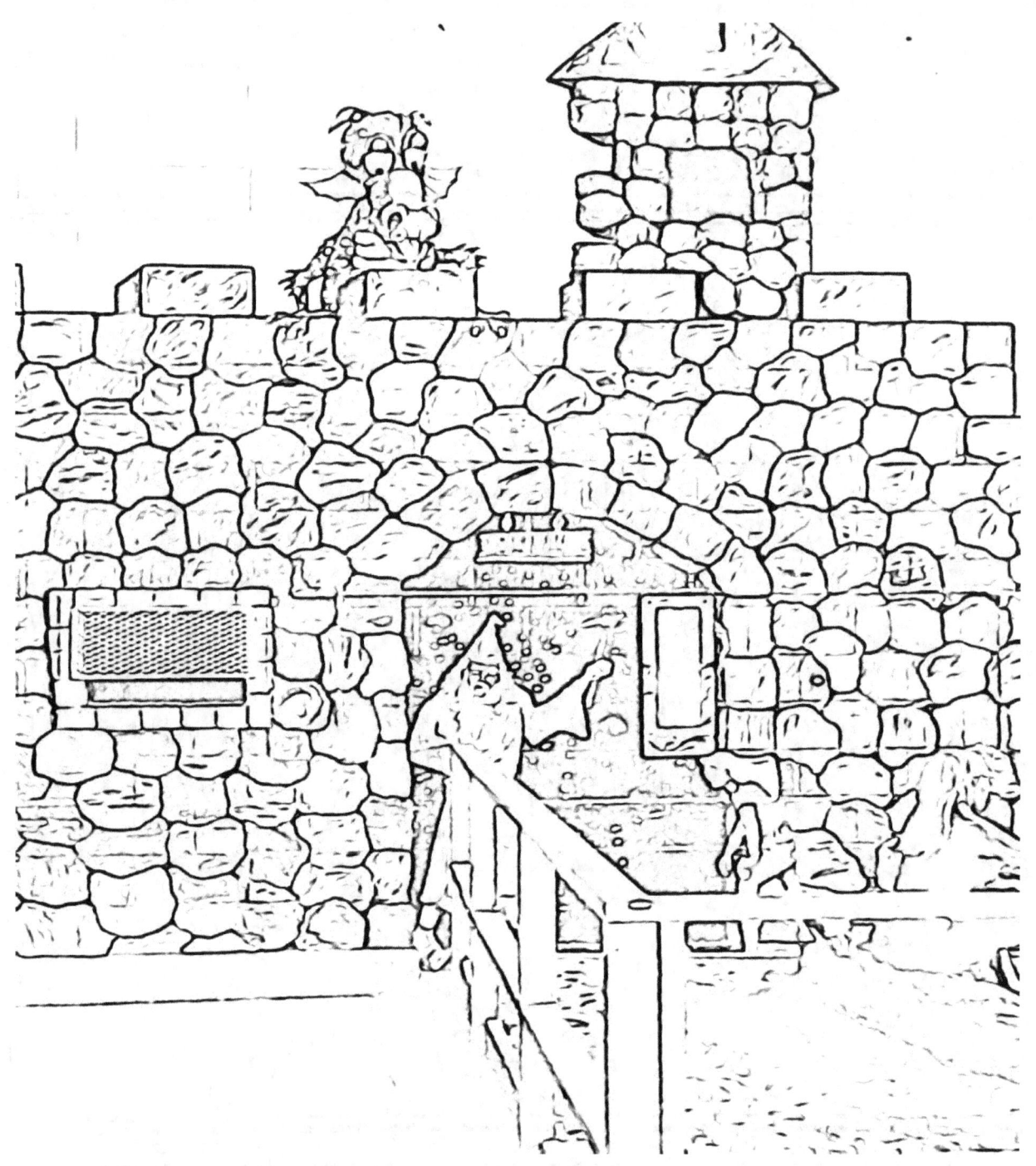

West Virginia Penitentiary

This mural in the Contact Visitation Room is of Merlin, a dragon, and a castle.

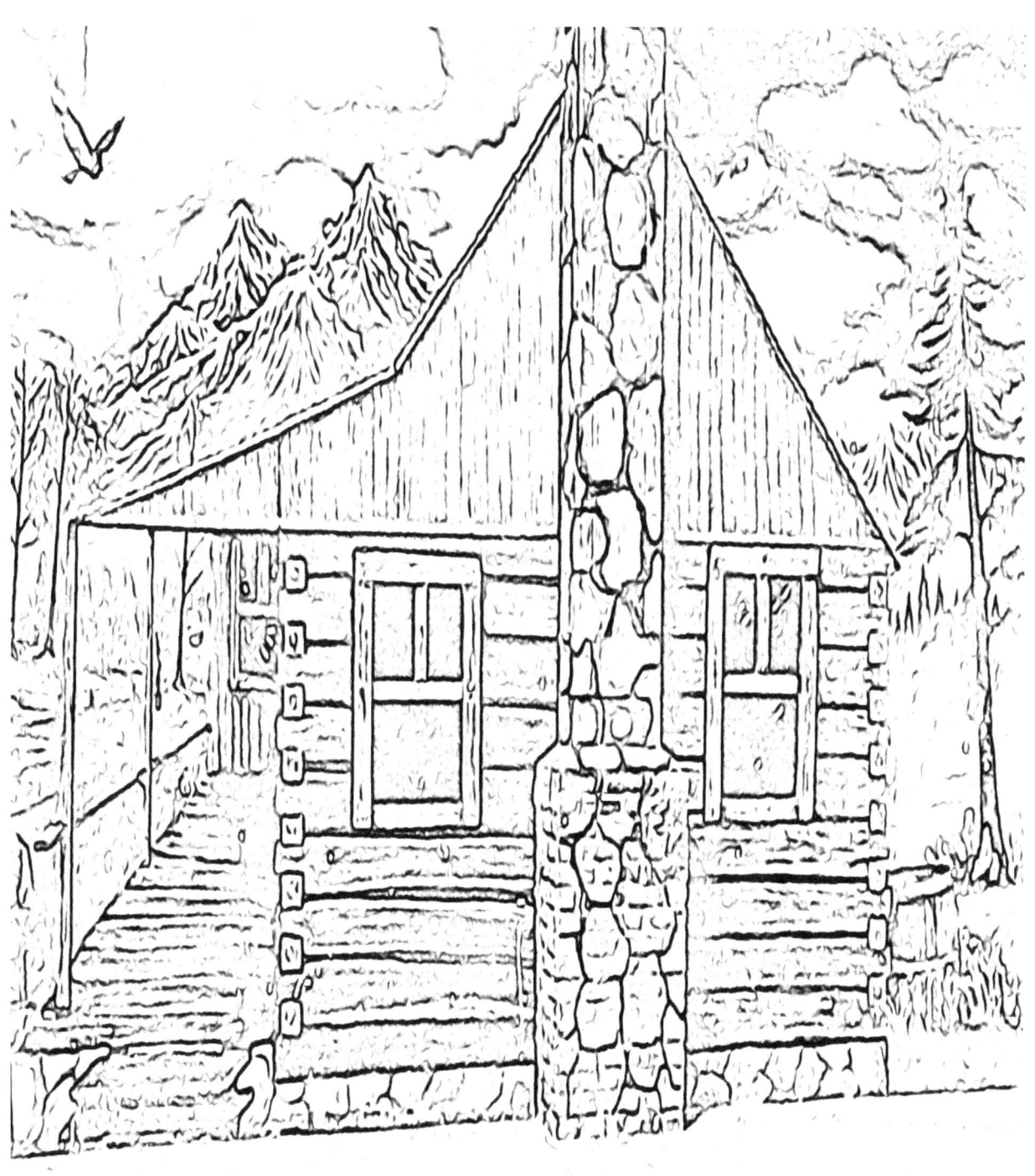

West Virginia Penitentiary

This mural in the Contact Visitation Room is of a log cabin.

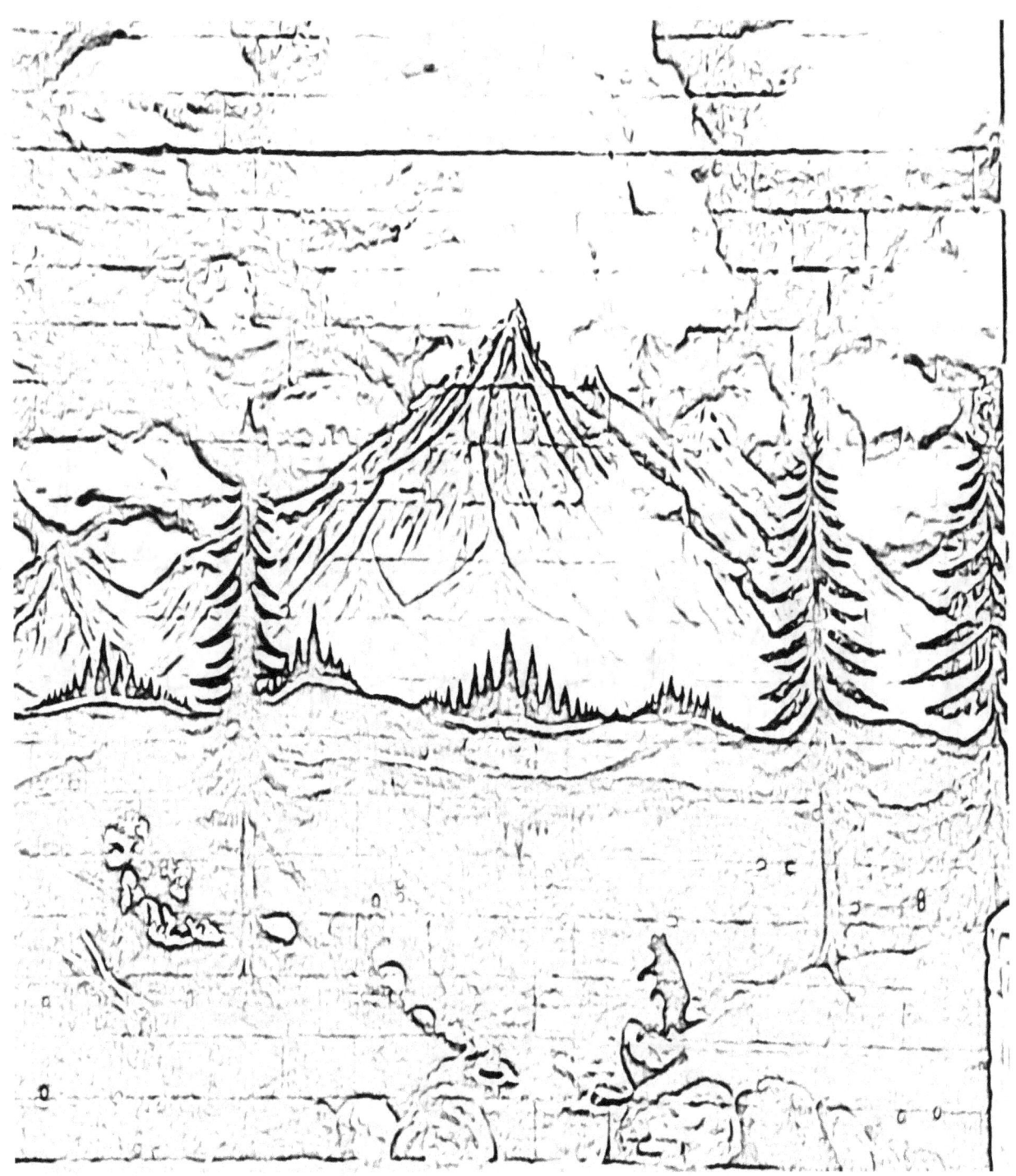

West Virginia Penitentiary

This mural in the Contact Visitation Room is of a mountain scene.

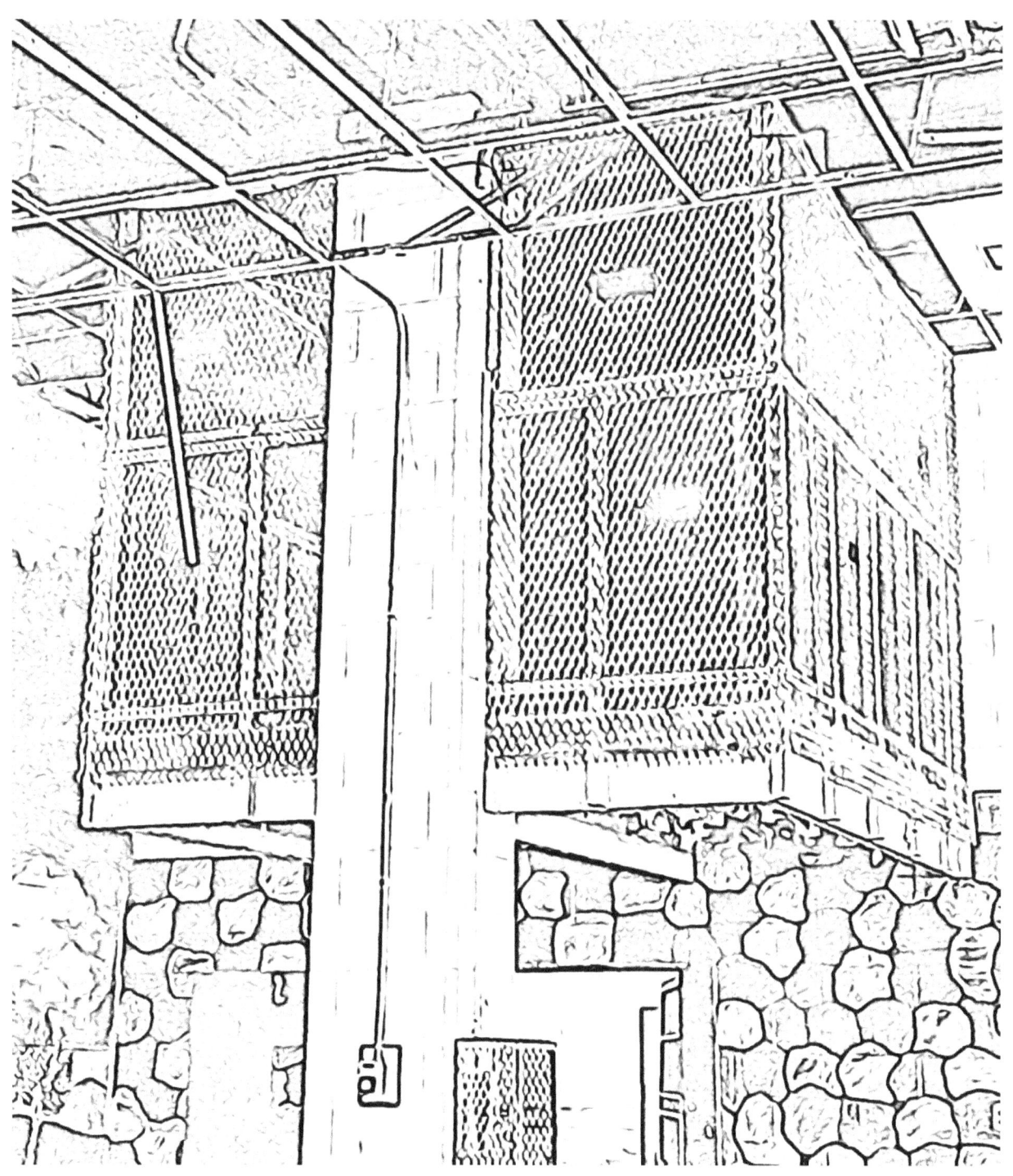

West Virginia Penitentiary

This is the gun cage in the Contact Visitation Room.

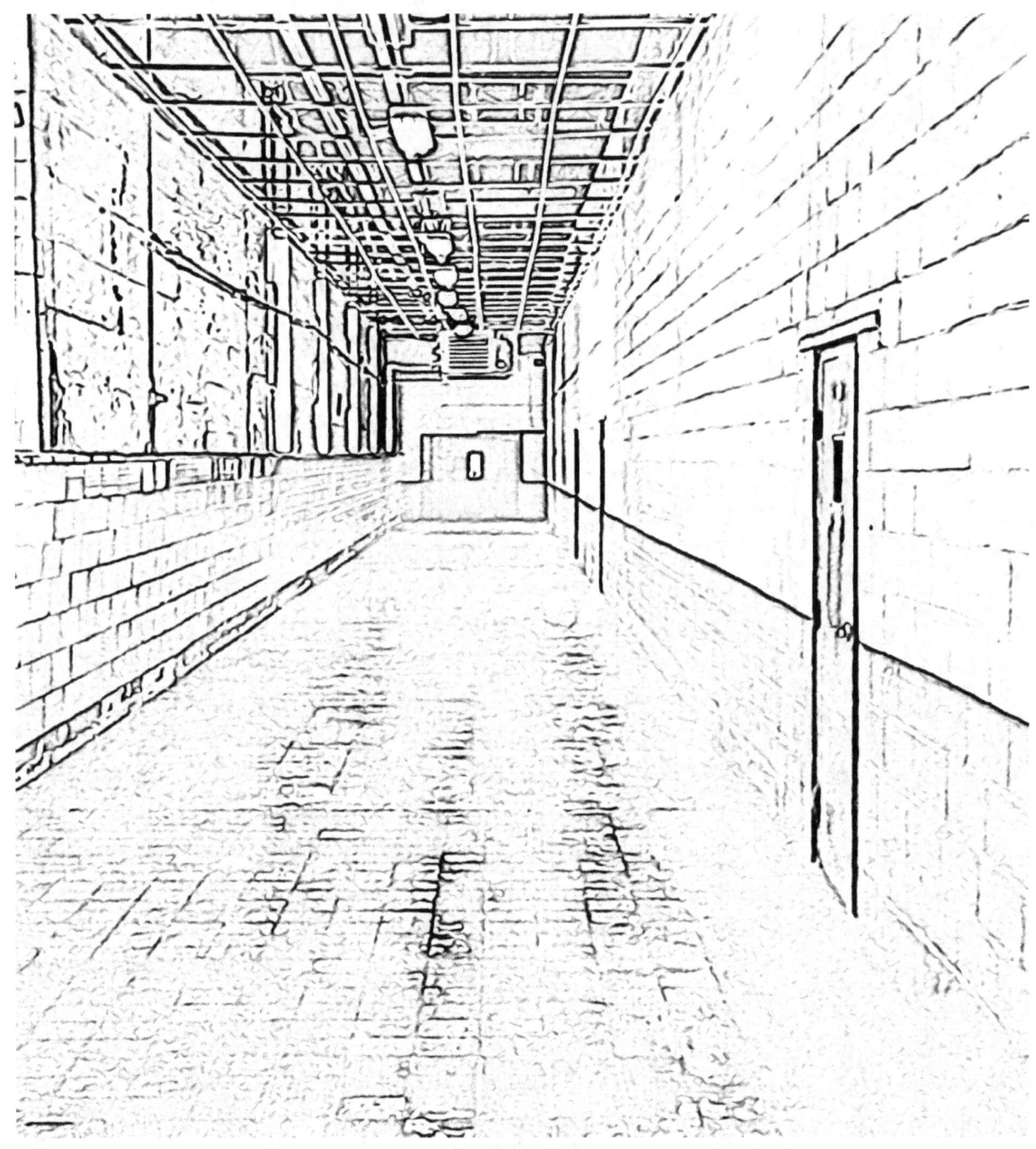

West Virginia Penitentiary

This is the hallway leading to the M.D.R. That stands for the Main Dining Room. The new Dining Room was built in March 1987.

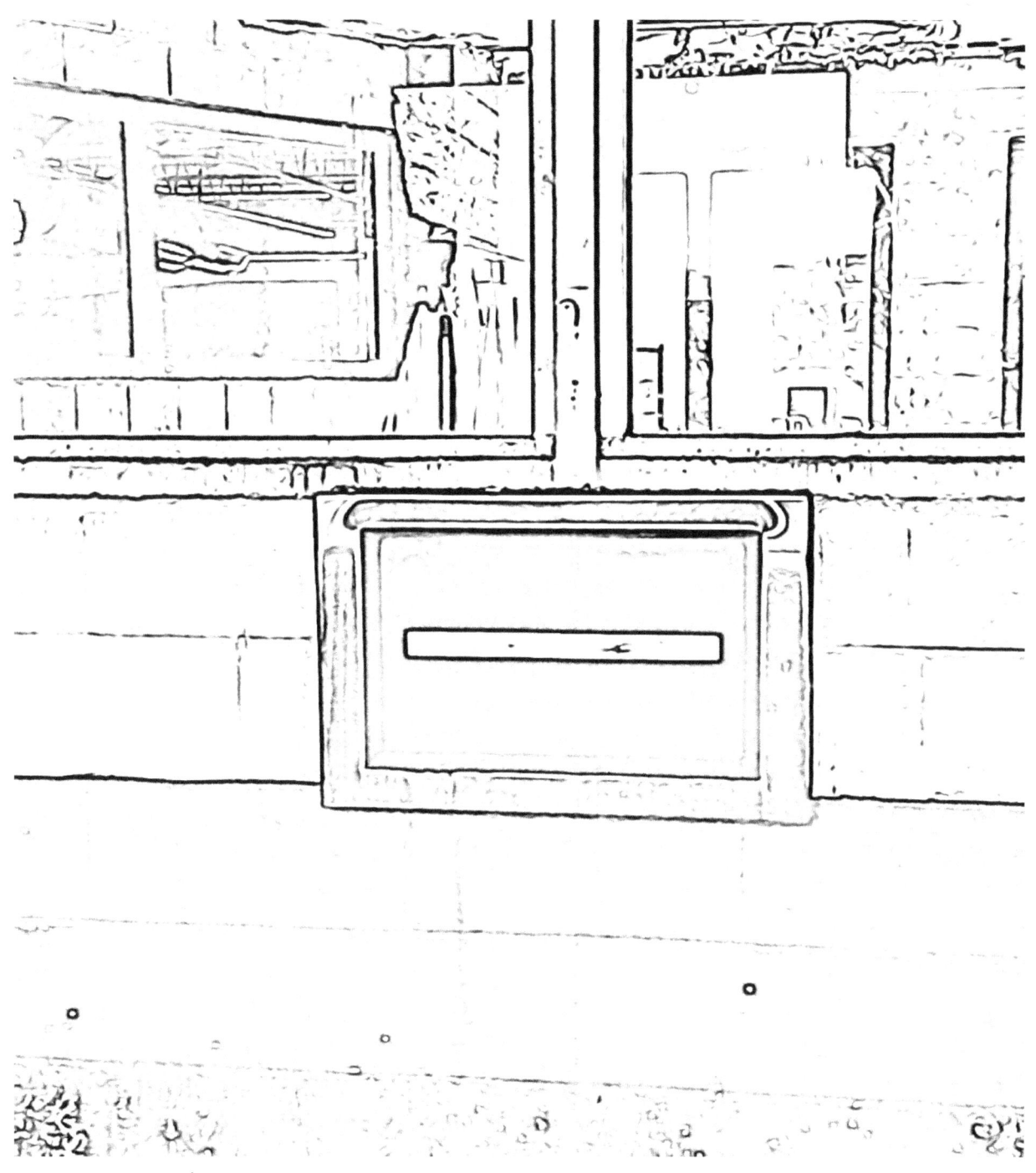

West Virginia Penitentiary

This is a drawer where medication was passed out to the inmates by a nurse. It is at the entrance into the M.D.R.

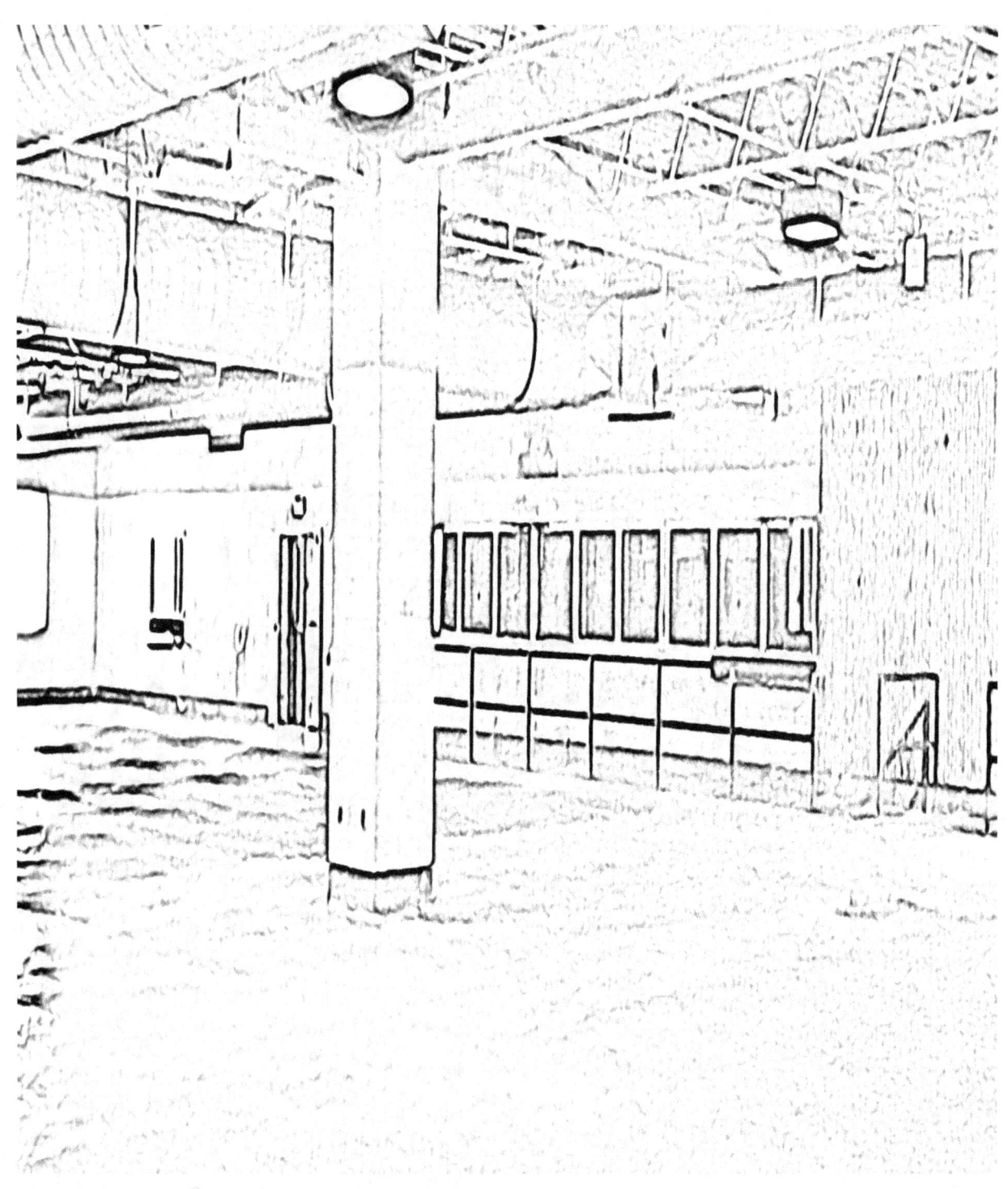

West Virginia Penitentiary

This is the new Dining Room. It was built after the 1986 riot

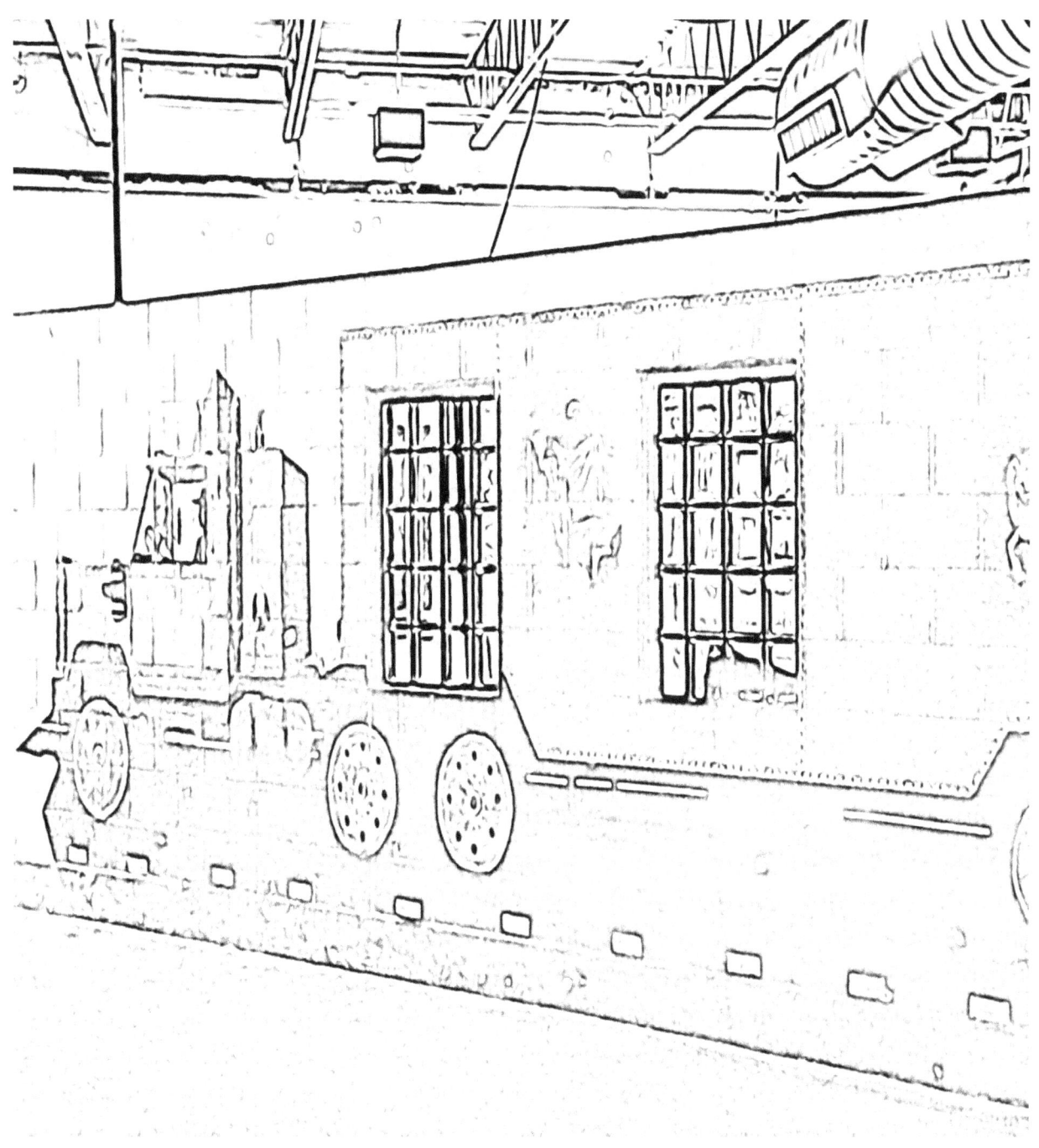

West Virginia Penitentiary

This is a mural in the new Dining Room. An inmate had once been a truck driver.

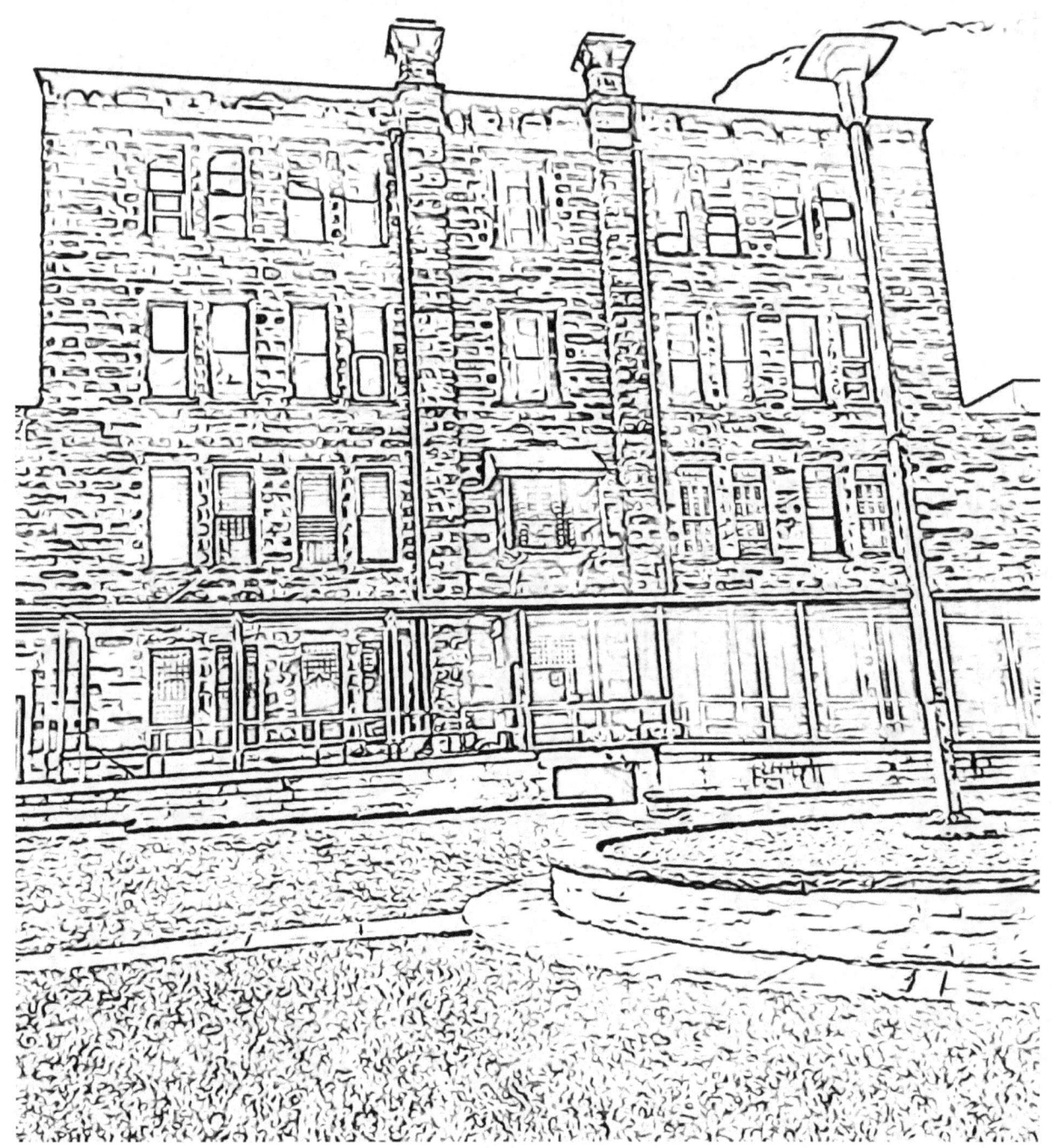

West Virginia Penitentiary

This is the original Administration area and Warden's Residence from the North Yard.

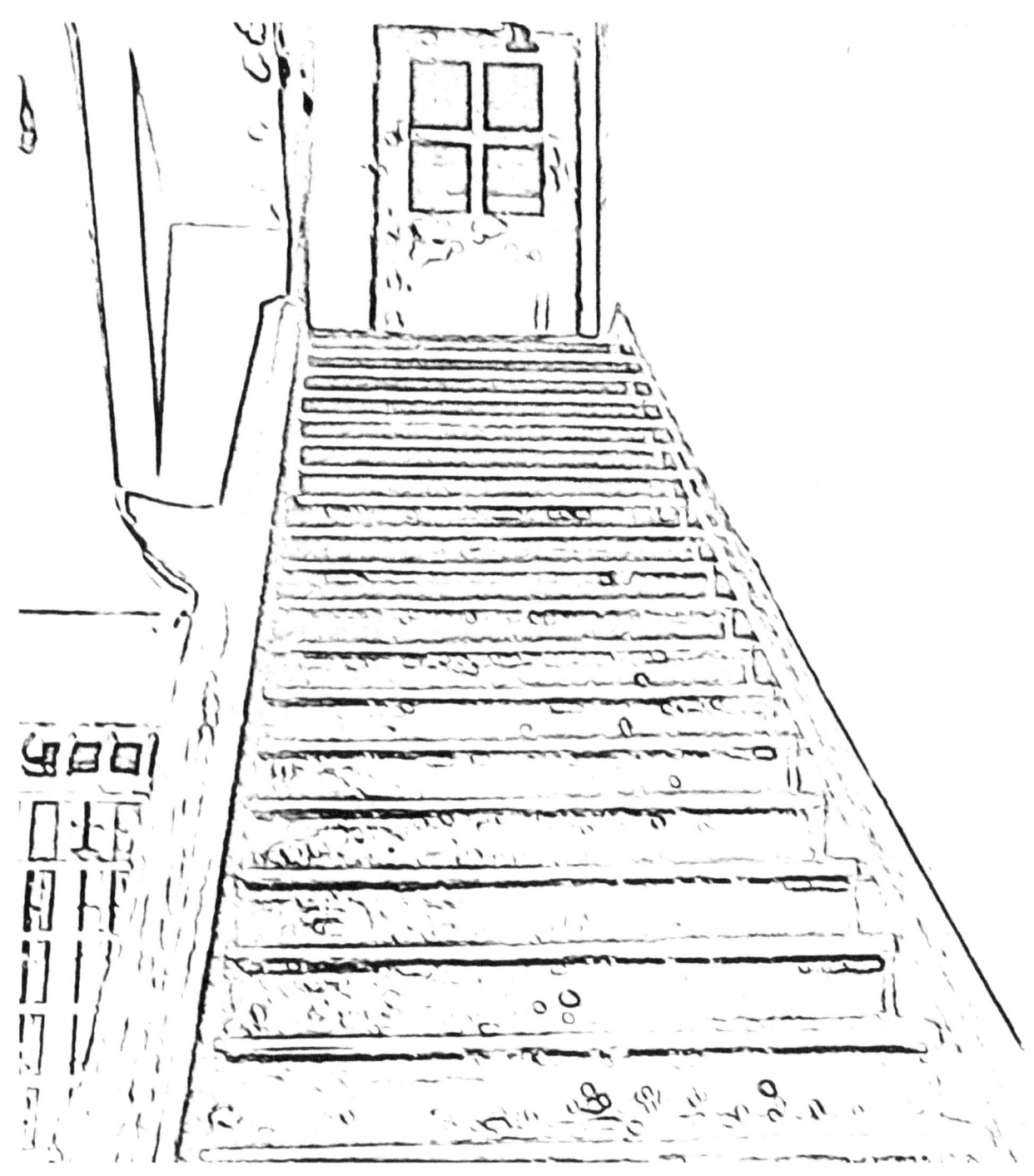

West Virginia Penitentiary

These were the only steps leading up to the Warden's office and his residence.

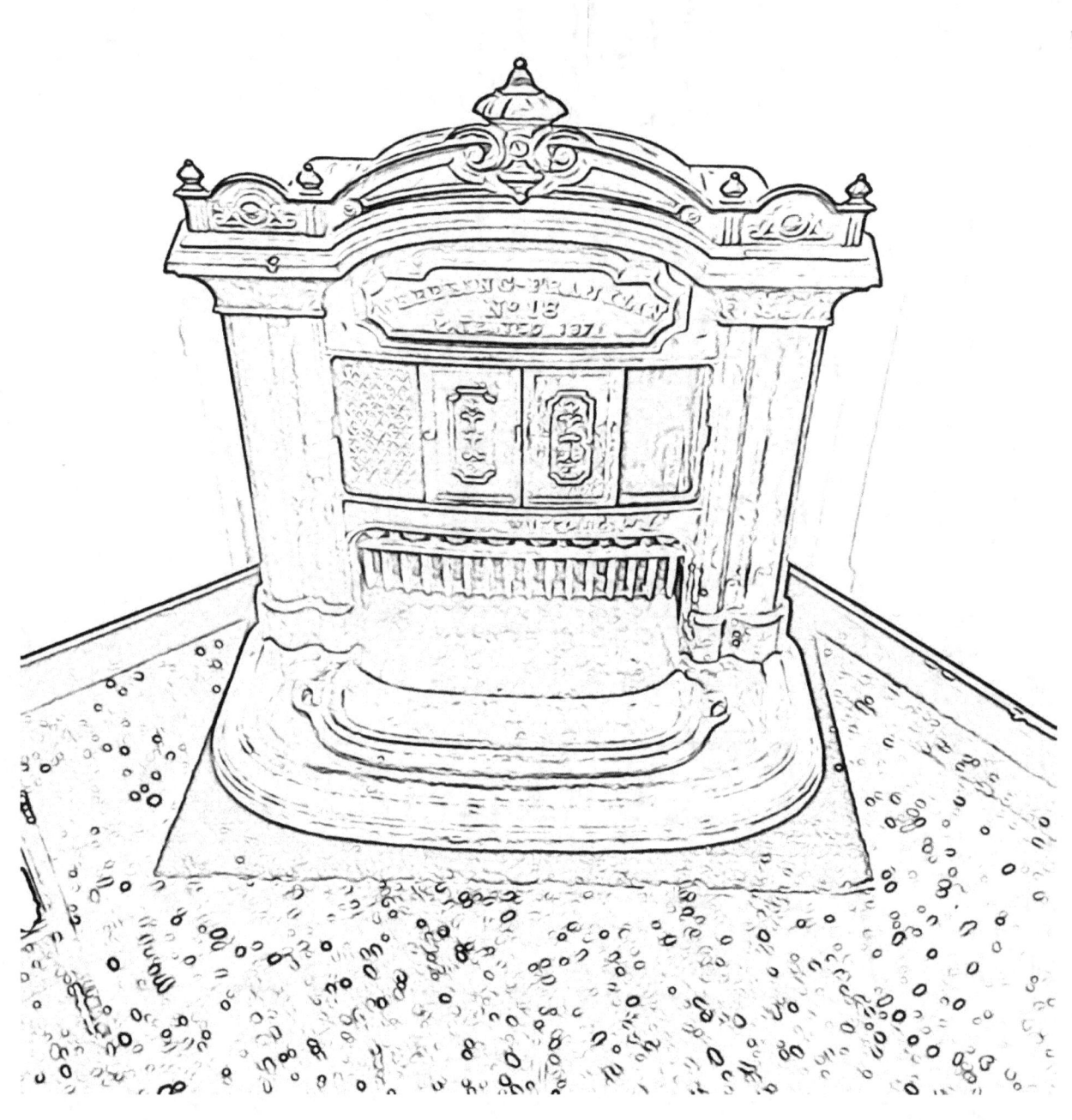

West Virginia Penitentiary

This is a wood burning stove that could have been used in the Warden's residence.

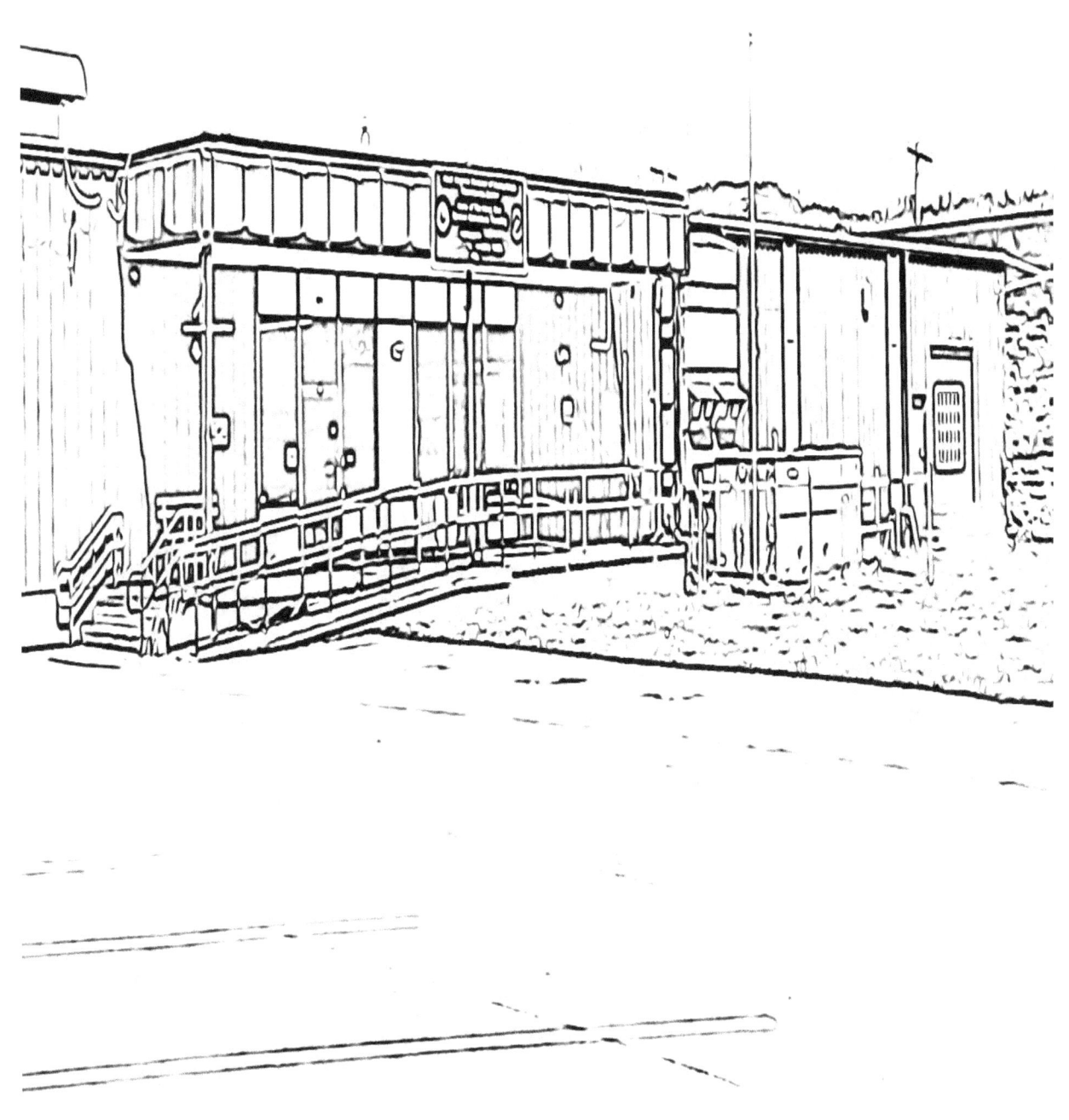

West Virginia Penitentiary

This is the Industries Building in the North Yard. Here the inmates learned trades, made products, and earned money for their commissary.

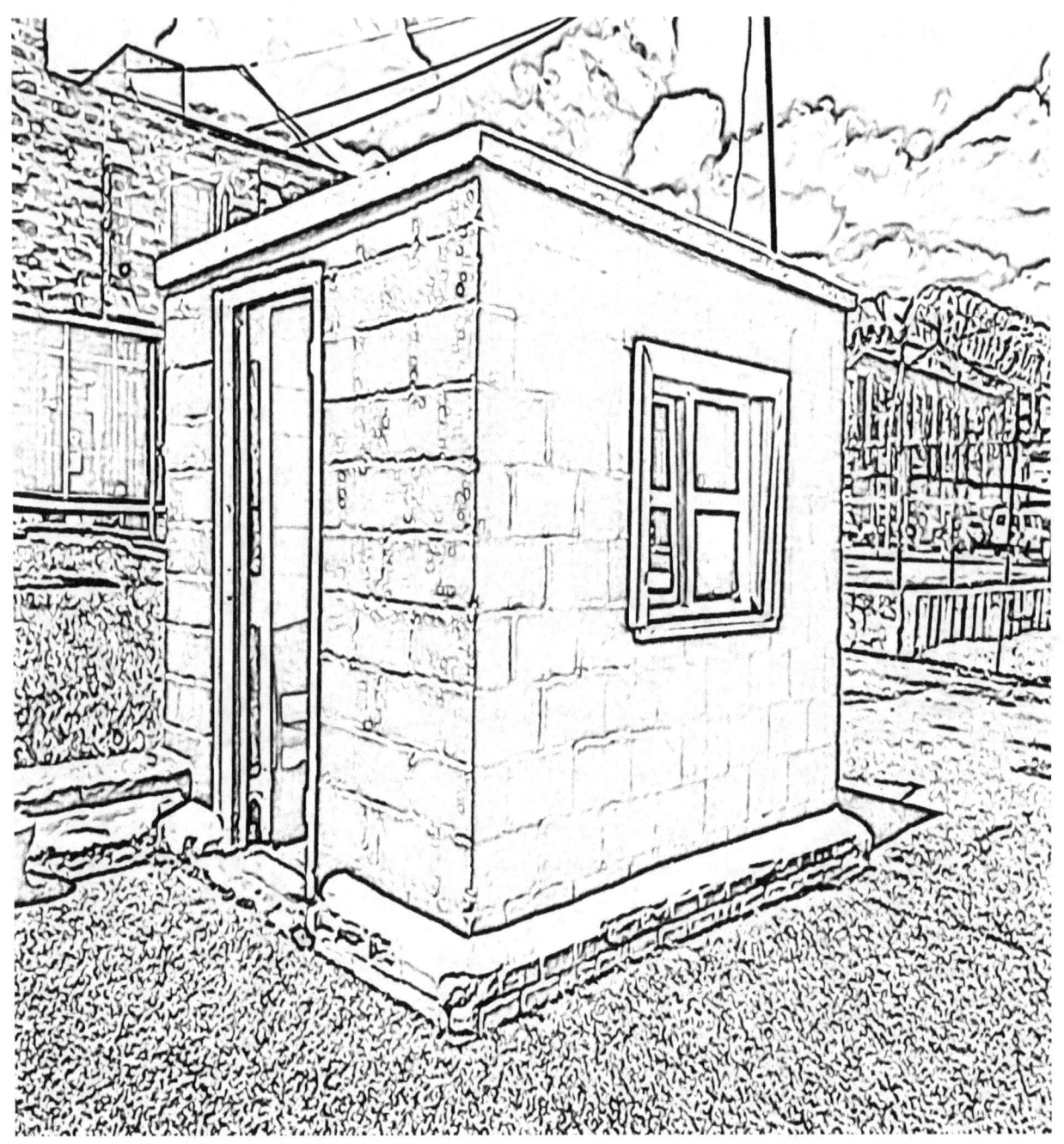

West Virginia Penitentiary

This is the guard shack in the North Yard. This is where the Correctional Officer could fill out paperwork.

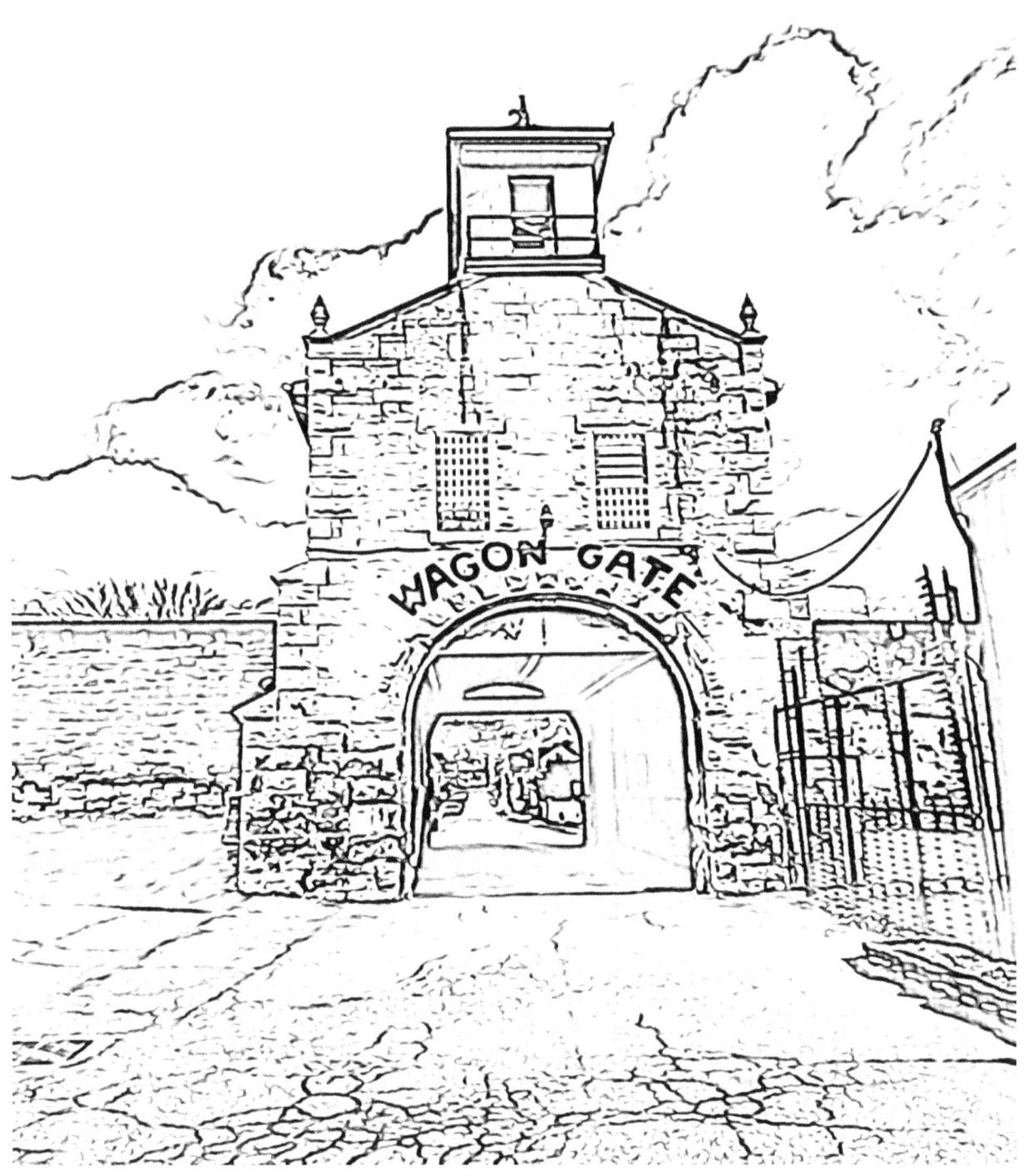

West Virginia Penitentiary

This is the North Wagon Gate. Inmates and supplies would come through this gate.

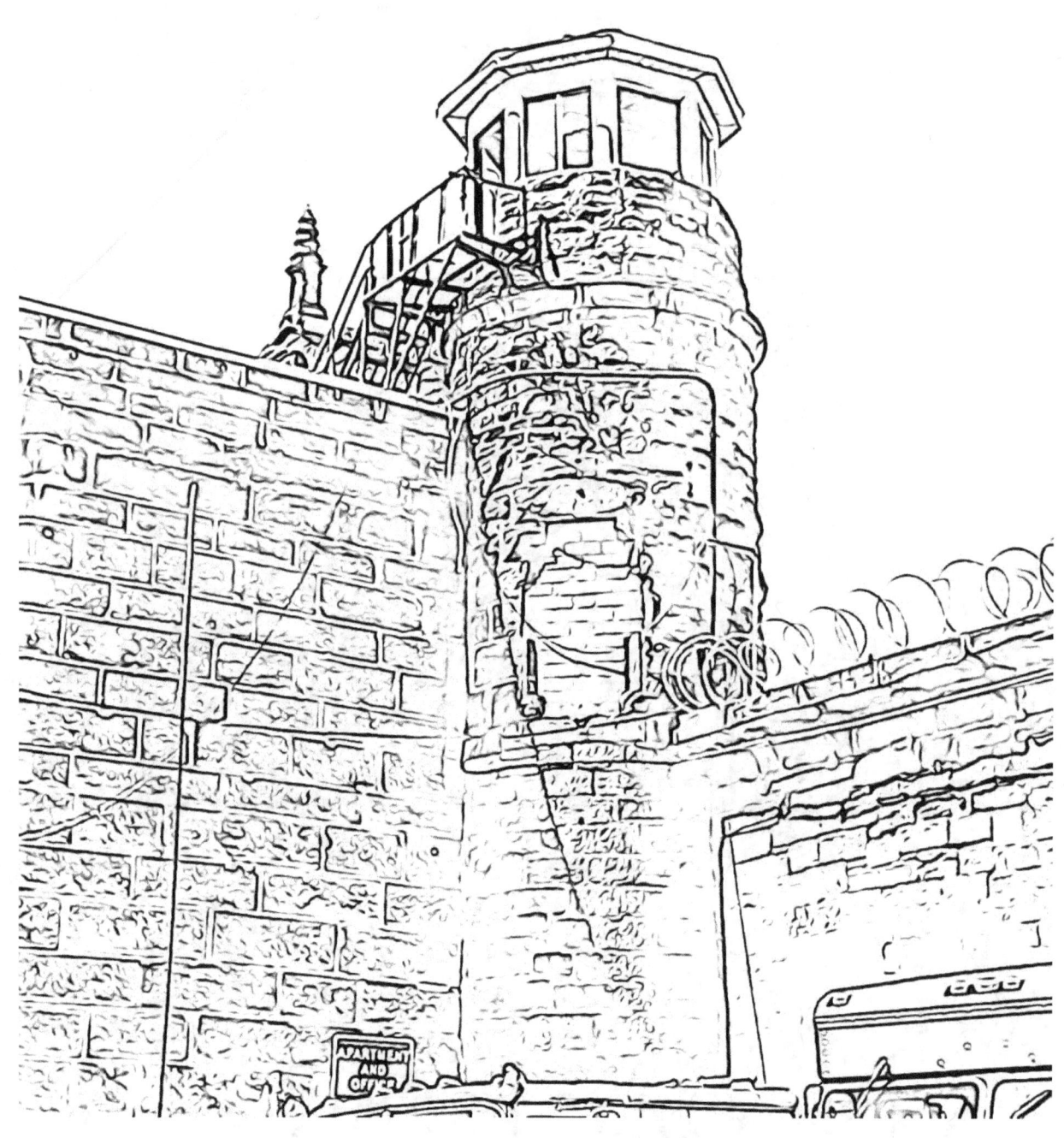

West Virginia Penitentiary

This is Tower 1 in the North Yard. A Correctional Officer watched over North Yard from here.

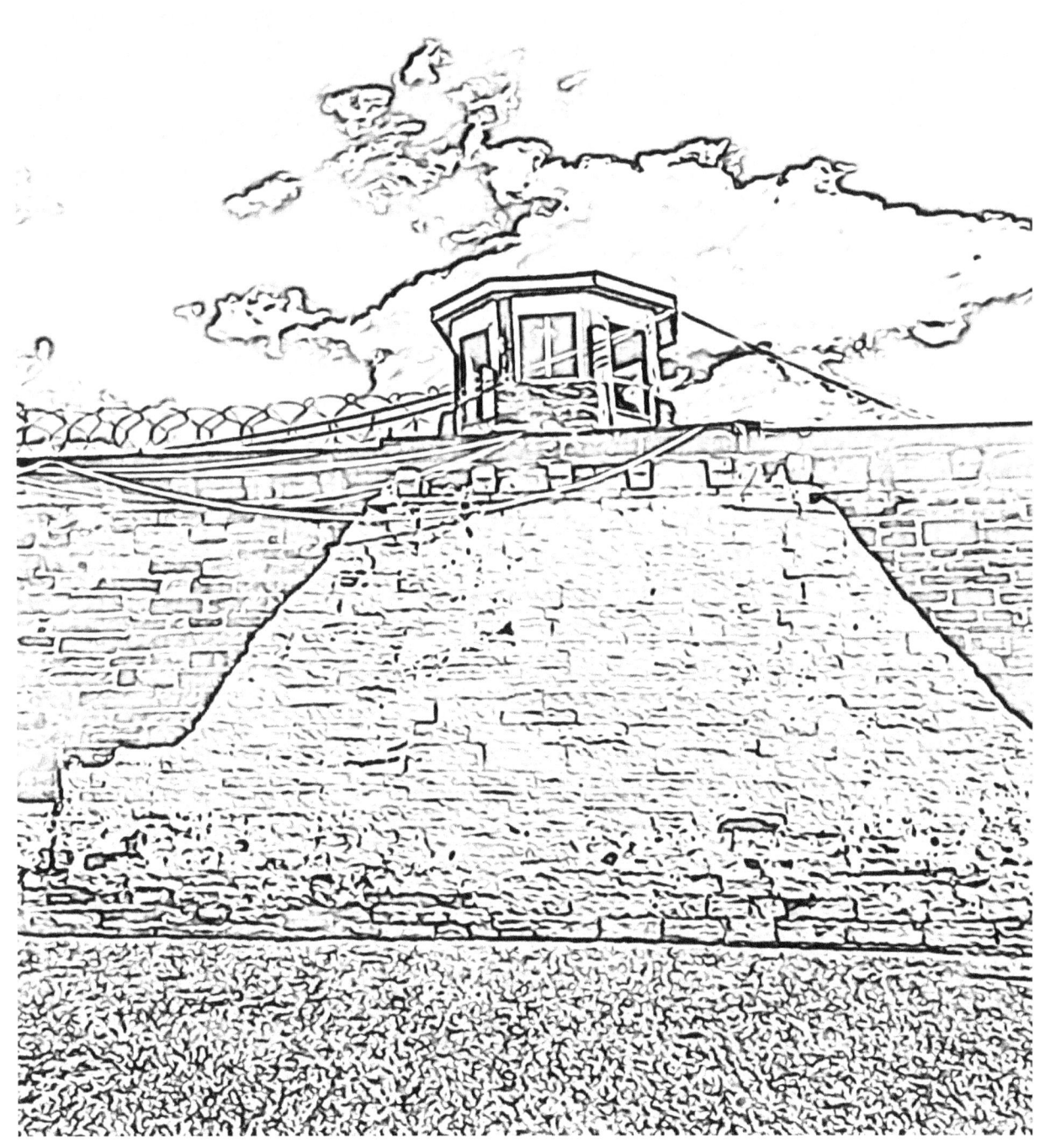

West Virginia Penitentiary

This is Tower 3 in the North Yard. A Correctional Officer watched over North Yard from here too.

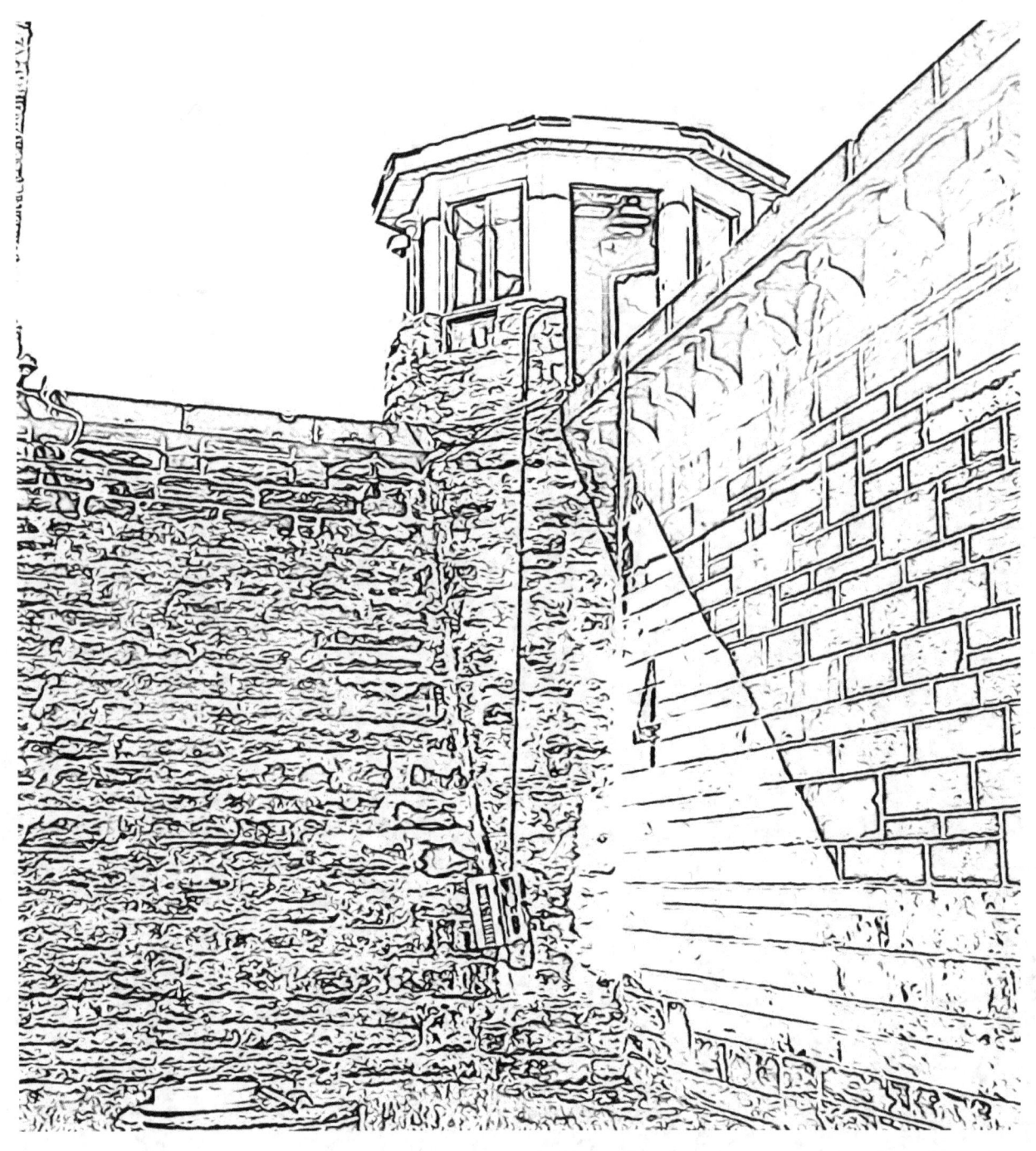

West Virginia Penitentiary

This is Tower 4. A Correctional Officer could watch over the North Yard and the South Yard from this tower.

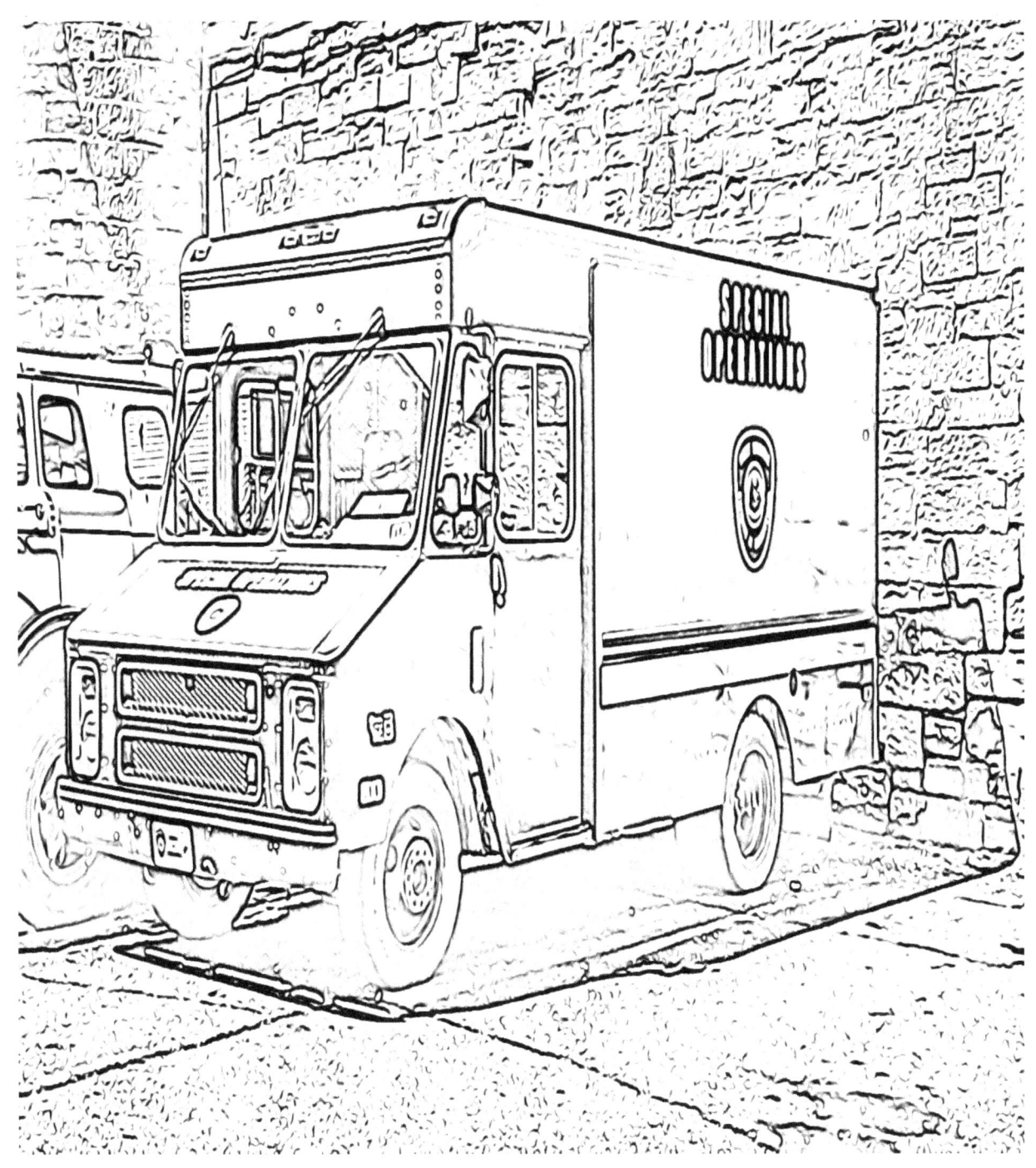

West Virginia Penitentiary

This was a van for Special Operations. It was used when the penitentiary was open.

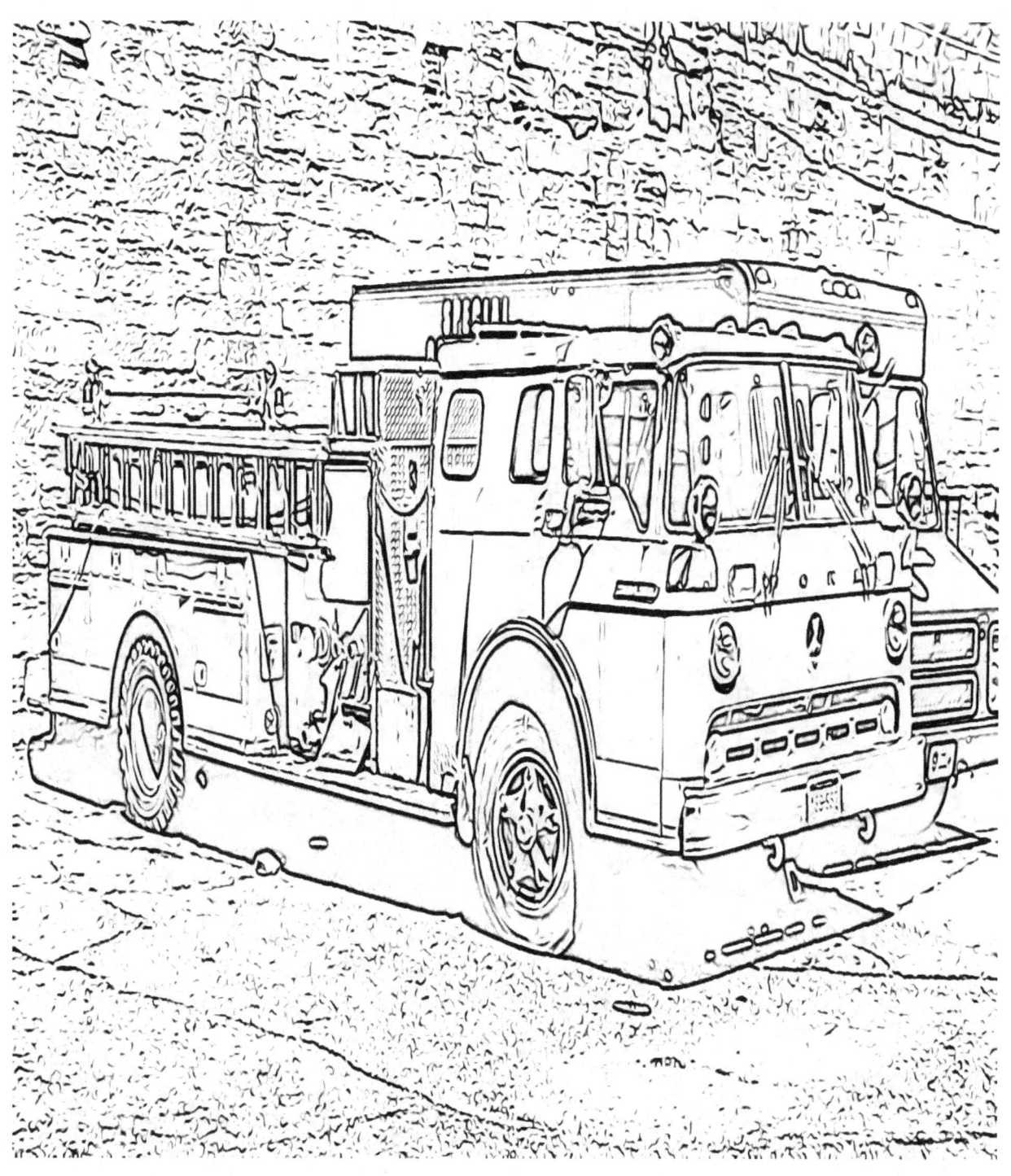

West Virginia Penitentiary

This is a fire engine. It was used when the penitentiary was open.

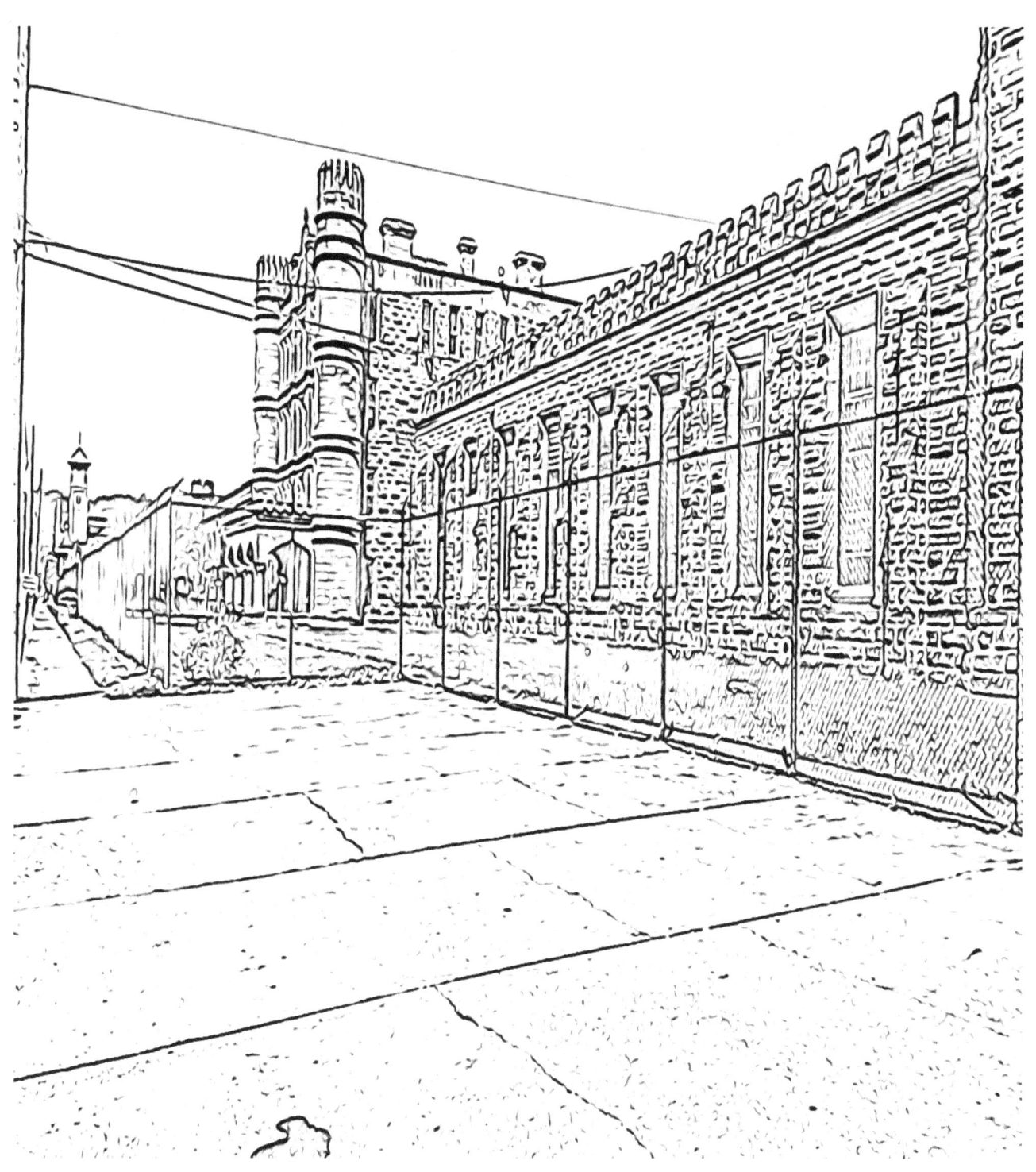

West Virginia Penitentiary

This is the front of the North Yard of the penitentiary.

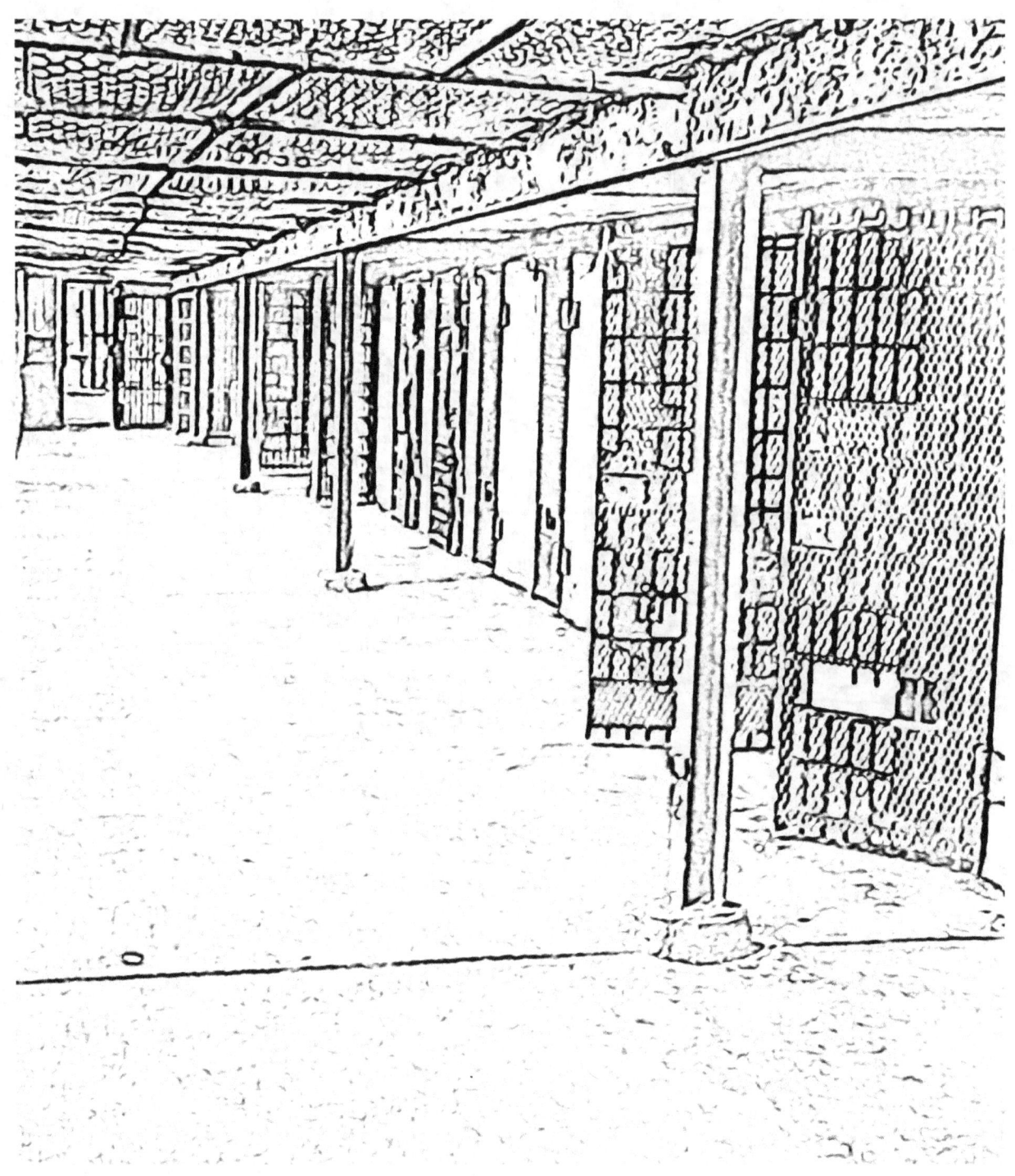

West Virginia Penitentiary

These are some of the cells in the North Hall.

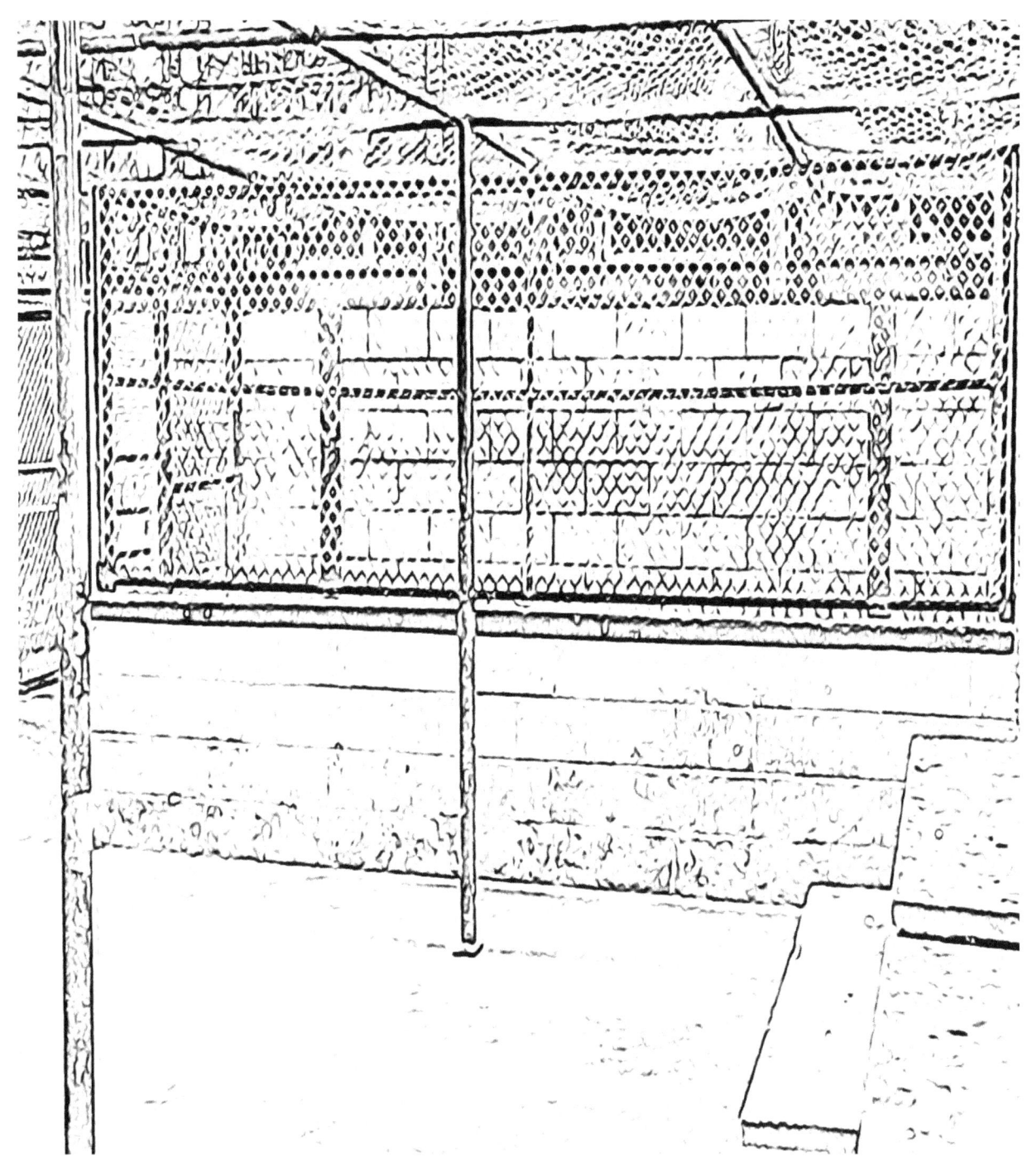

West Virginia Penitentiary

This is the shower area in the North Hall. The inmates would shower four at a time.

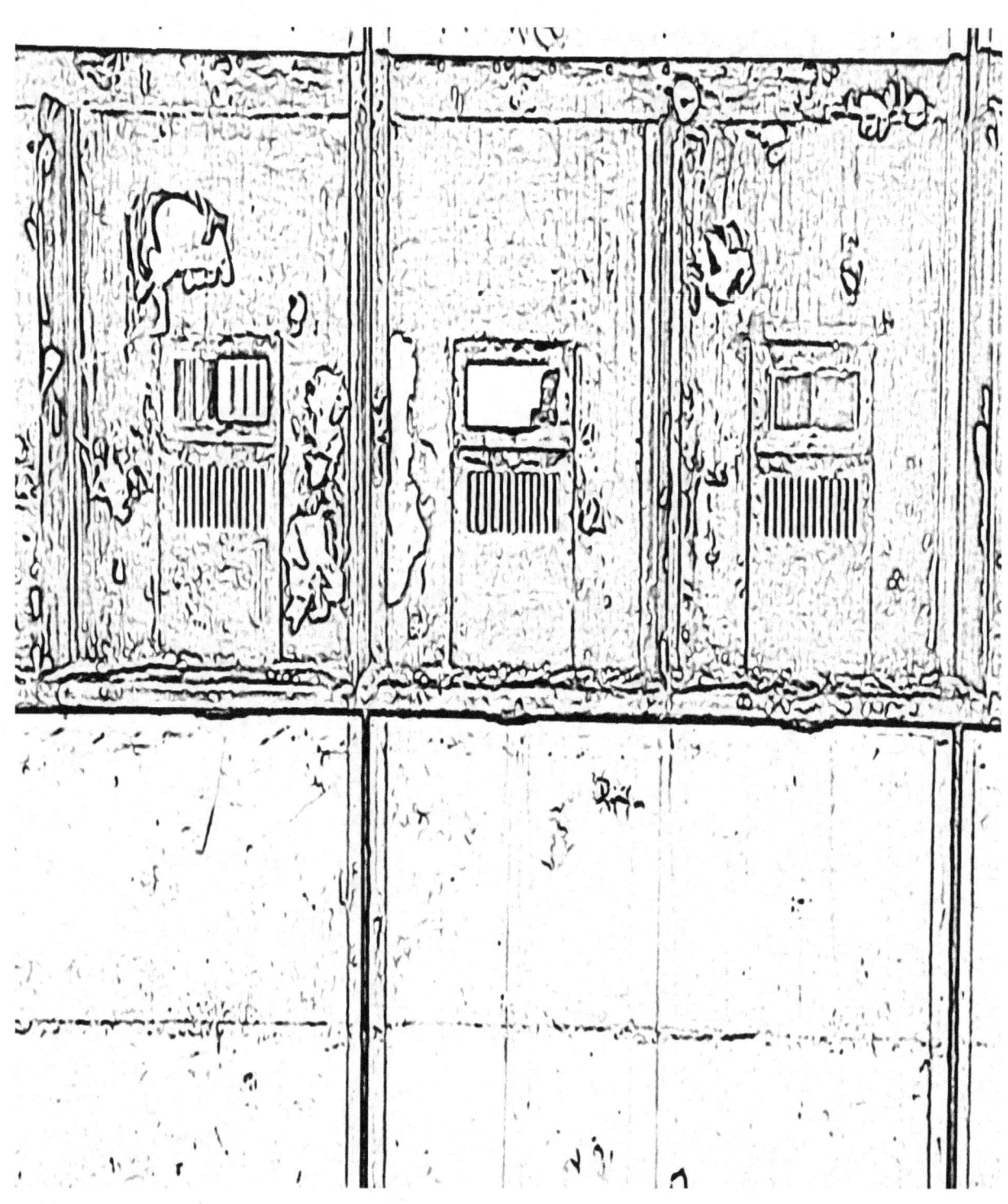

West Virginia Penitentiary

This was the Non-Contact Visitation Room for the North Hall inmates.

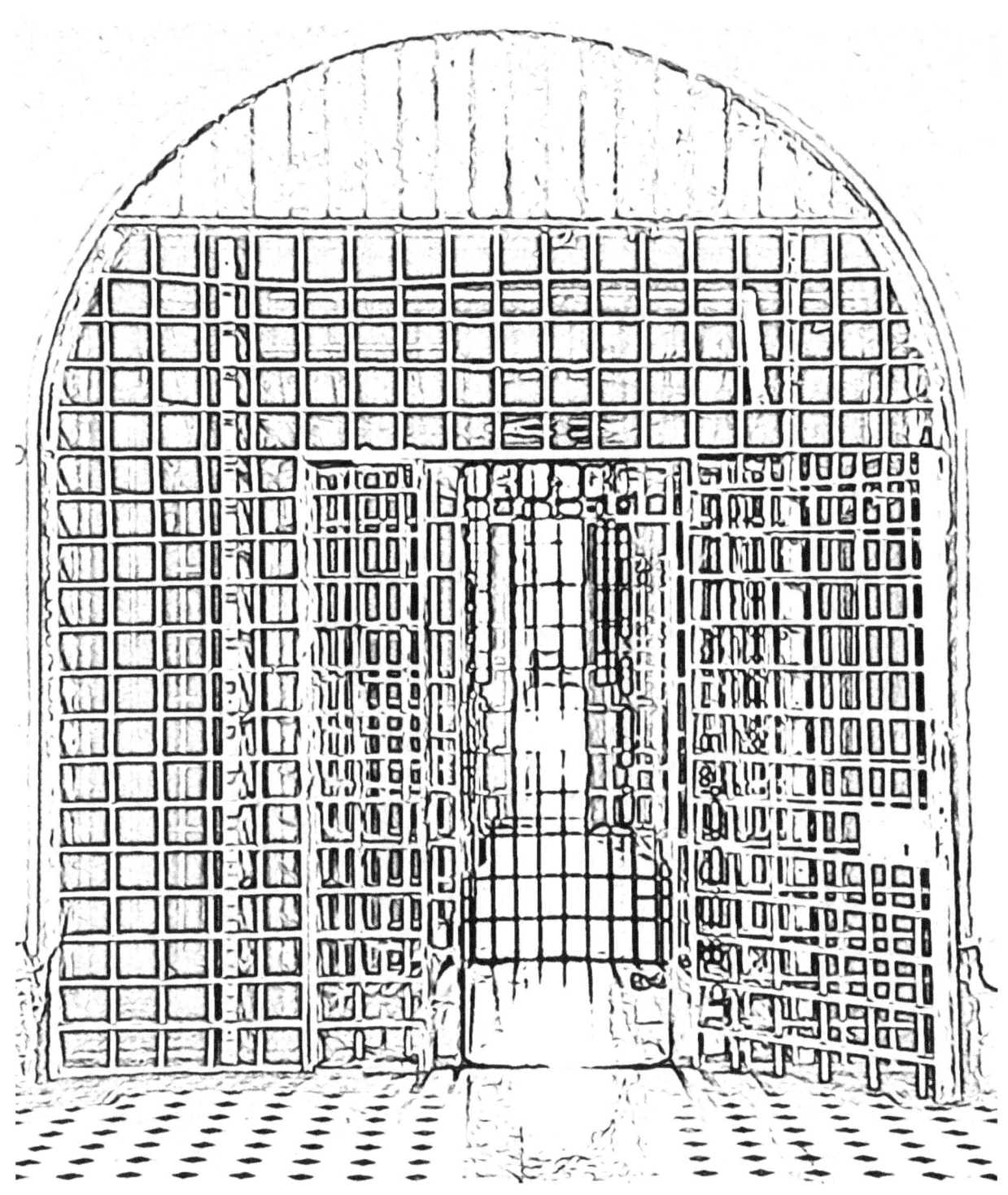

West Virginia Penitentiary

This was the "Wheel". It was built here in 1890's.

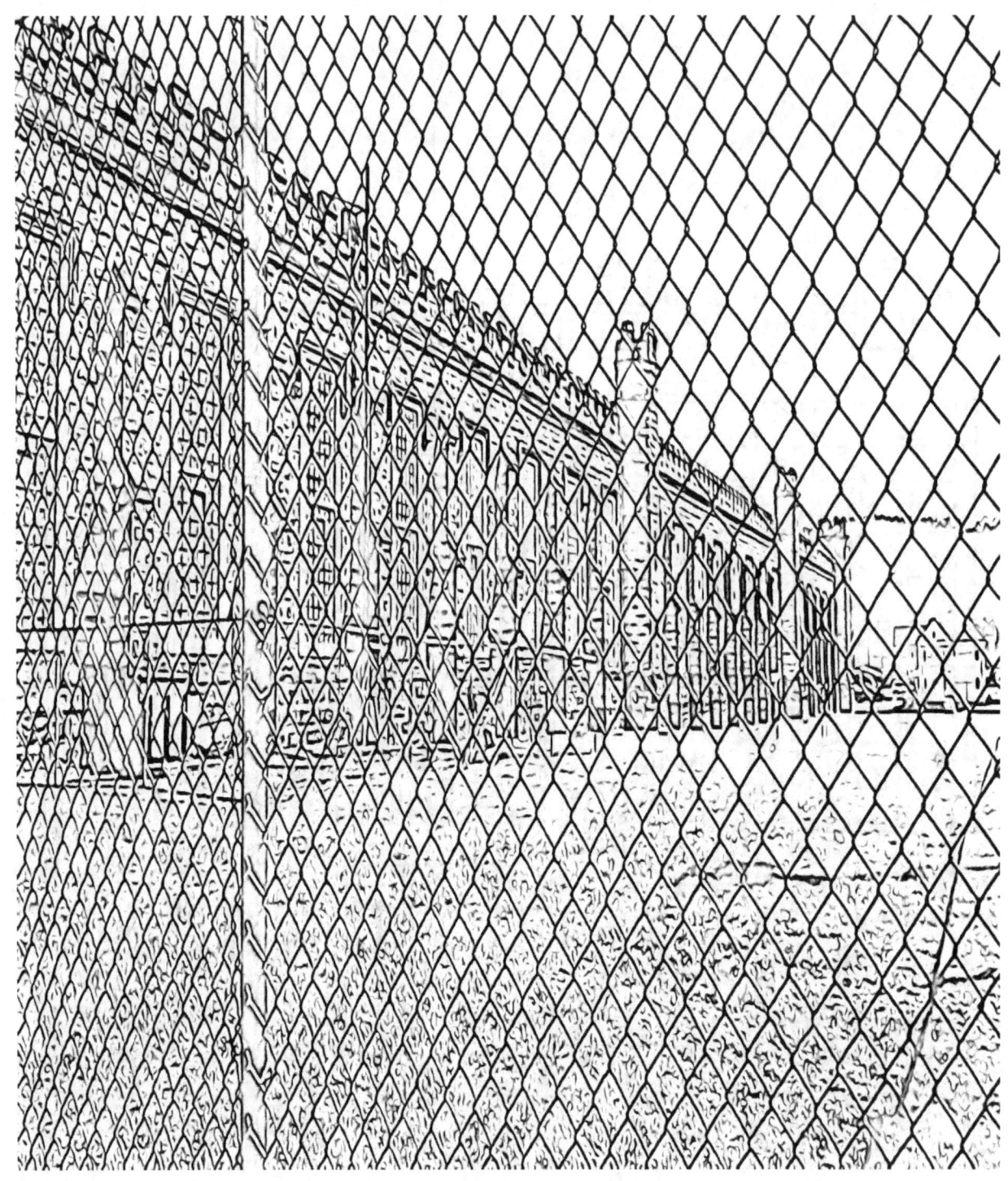

West Virginia Penitentiary

This is the front of the South Yard of the penitentiary.

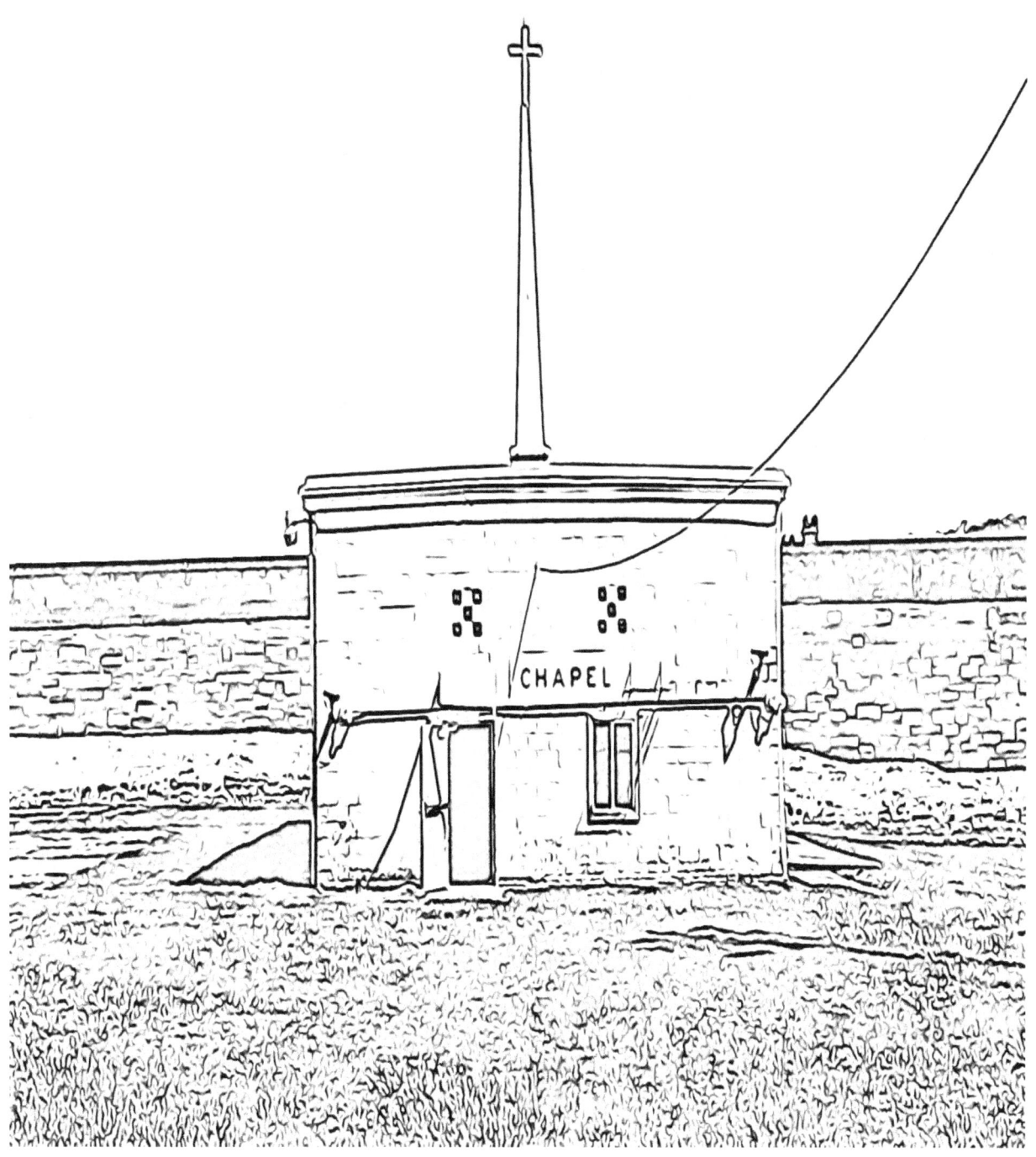

West Virginia Penitentiary

This is the chapel in the South Yard.

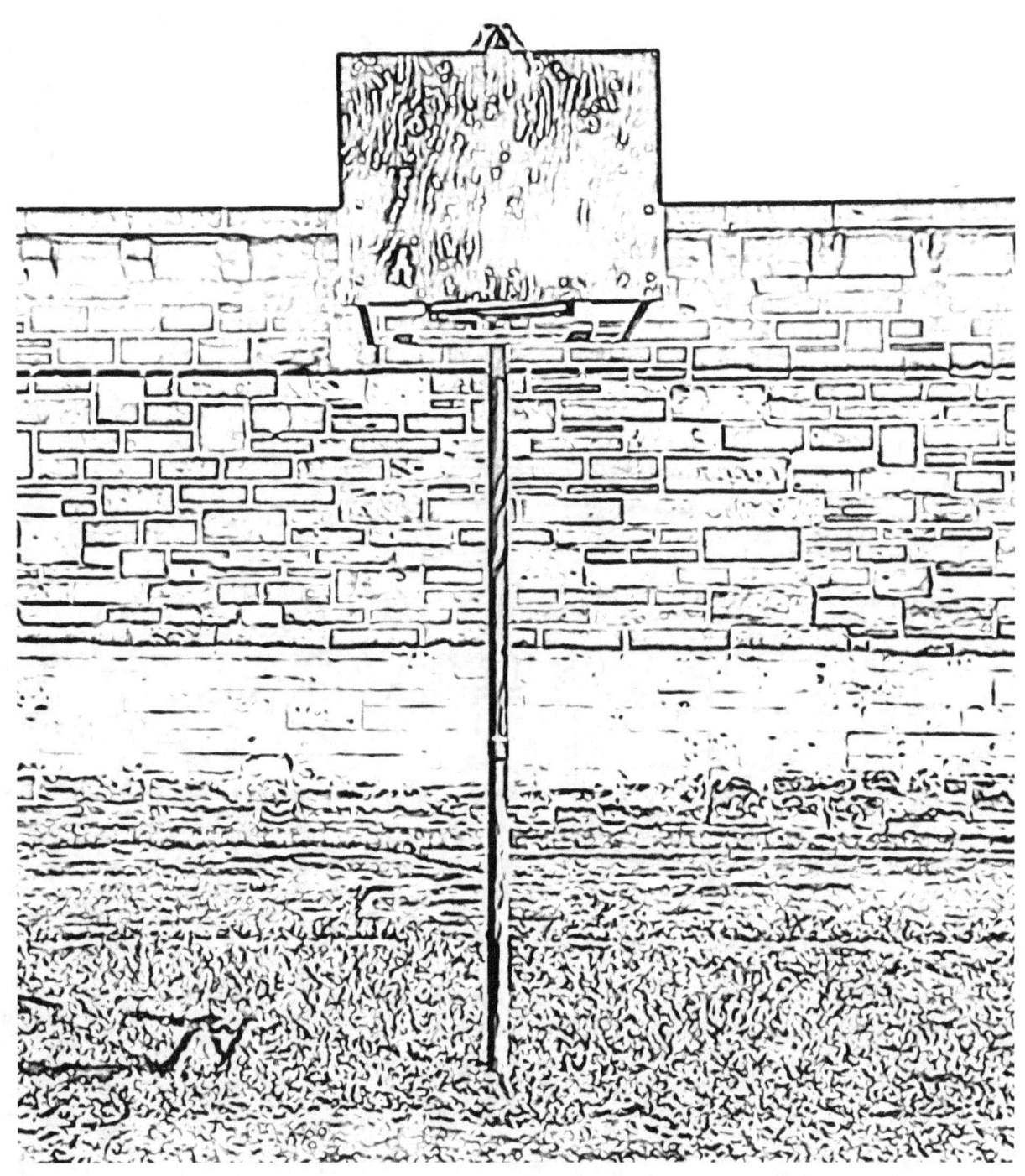

West Virginia Penitentiary

This is a basketball hoop in the South Yard.

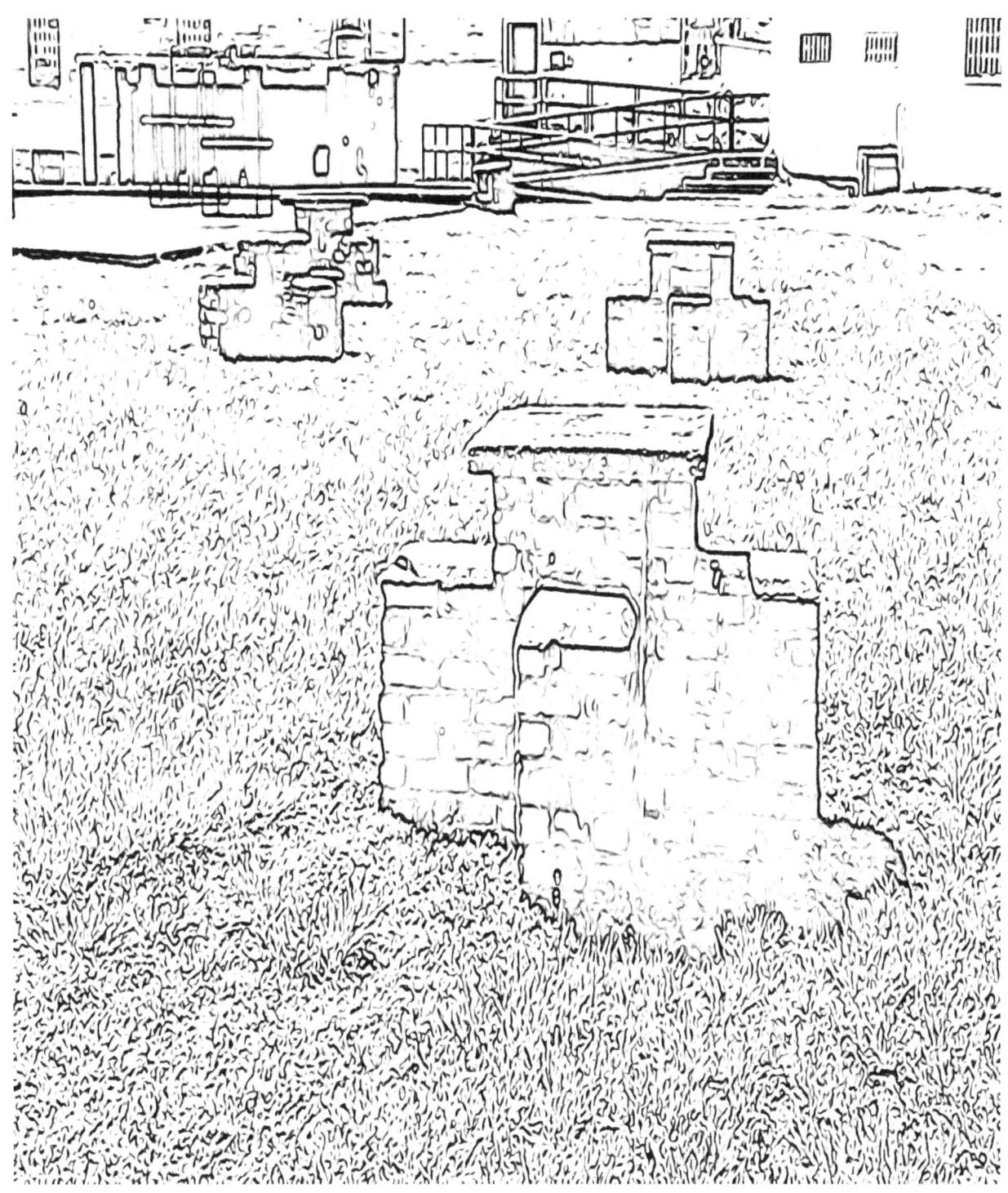

West Virginia Penitentiary

These were some of the tables in the South Yard.

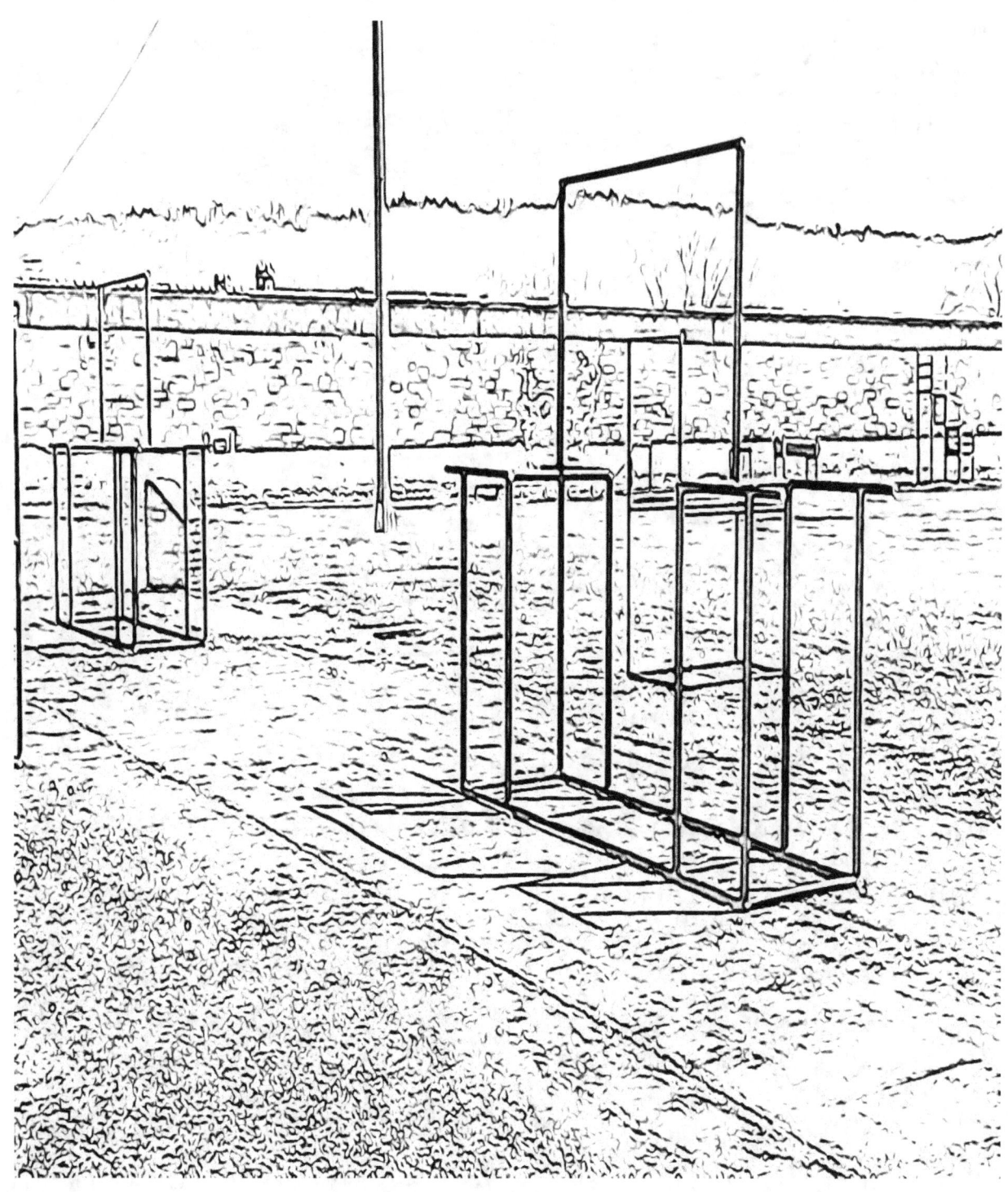

West Virginia Penitentiary

This was the weightlifting area in the South Yard.

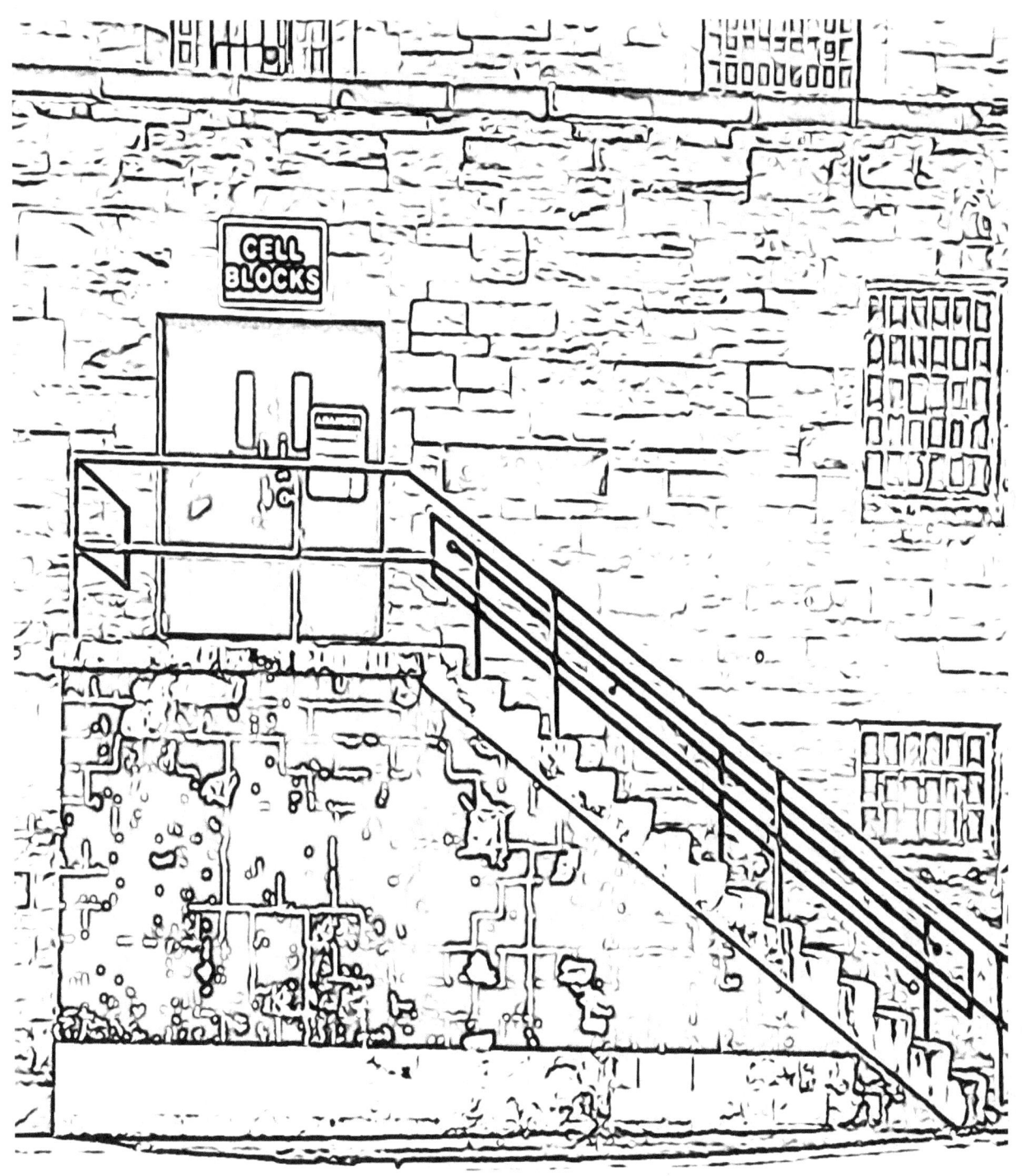

West Virginia Penitentiary

These were steps to the cell blocks in the South Yard.

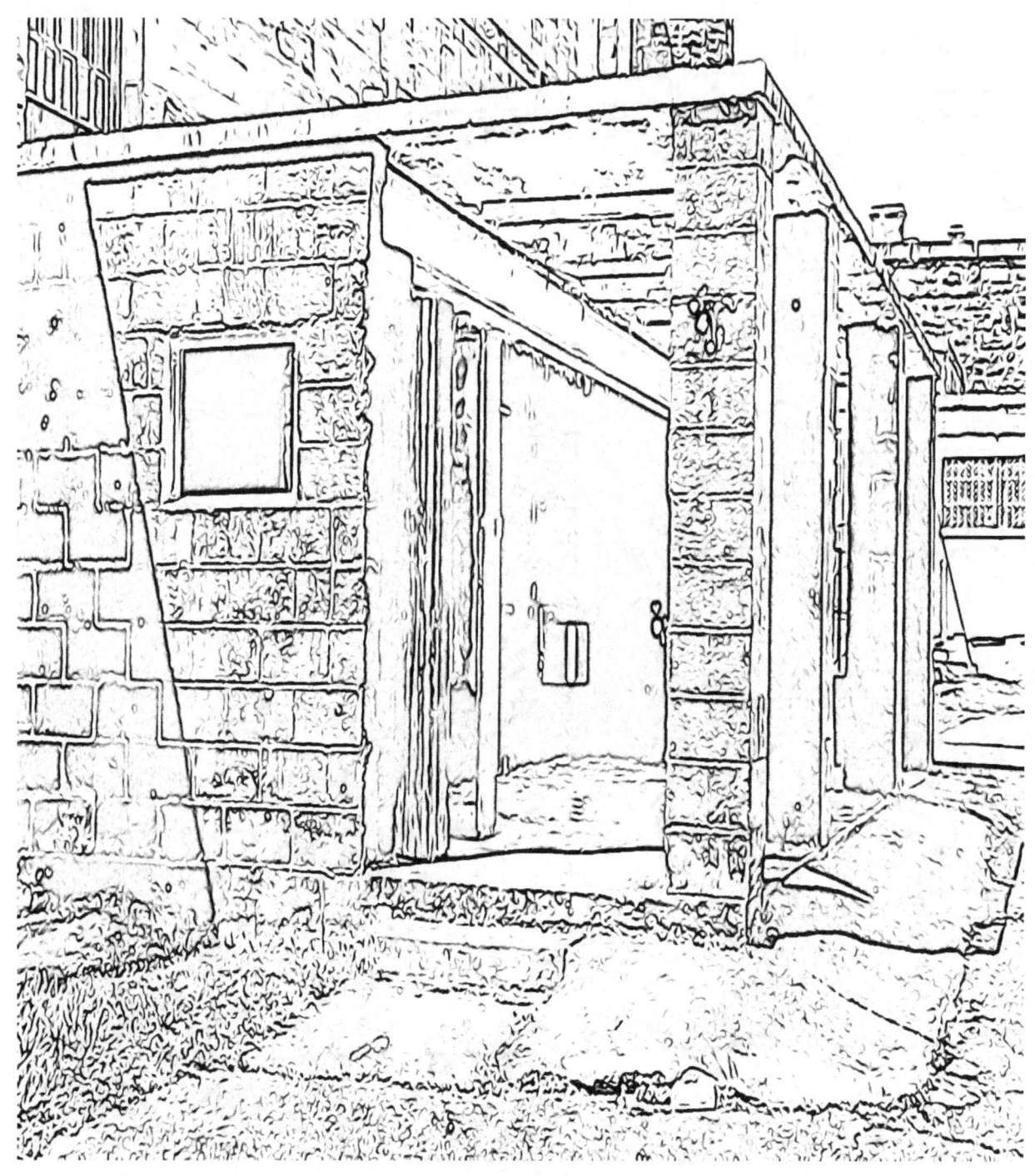

West Virginia Penitentiary

This was the toilet area in the South Yard.

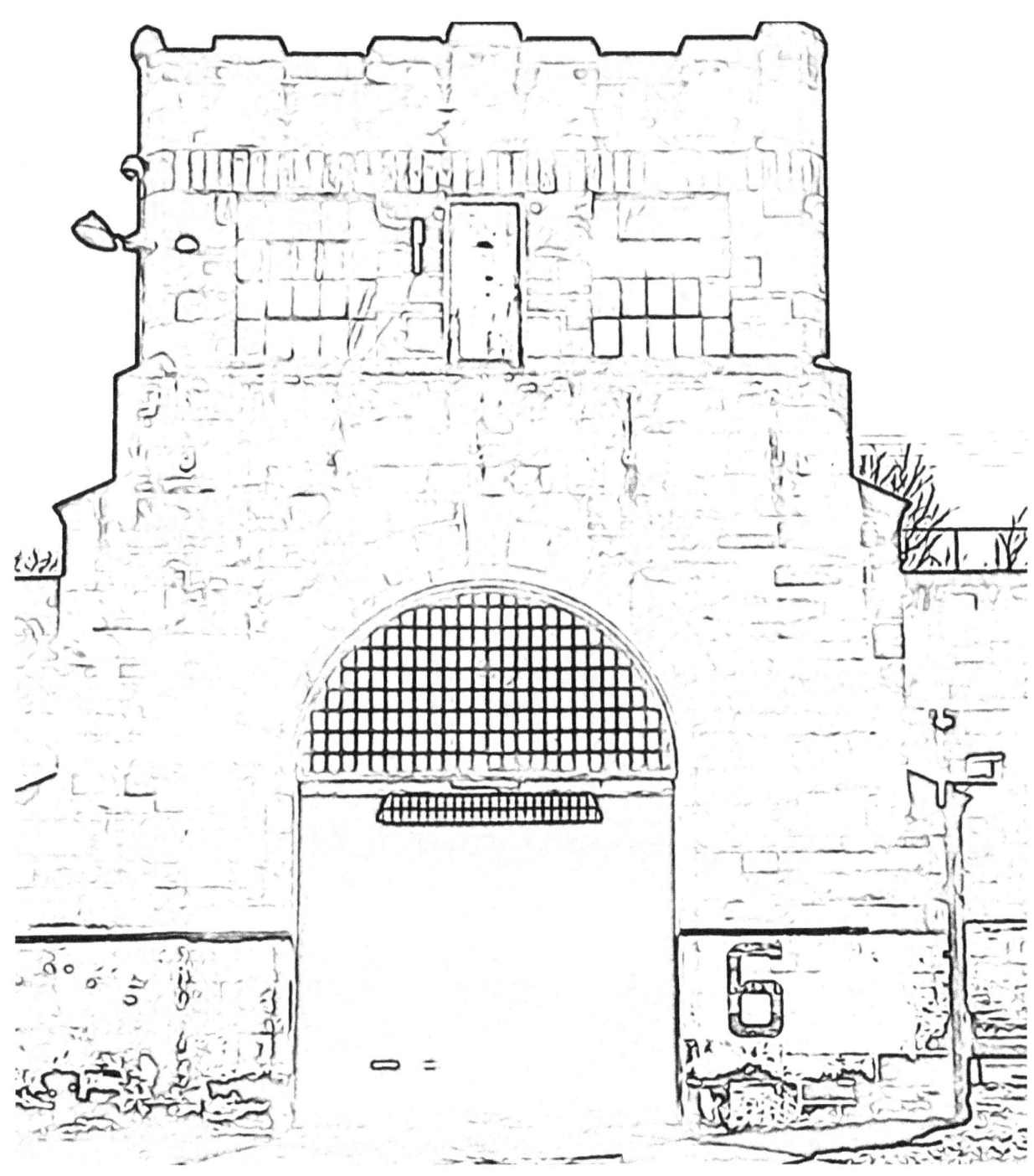

West Virginia Penitentiary

This was the South Wagon Gate in the South Yard. On top, it was Tower 6.

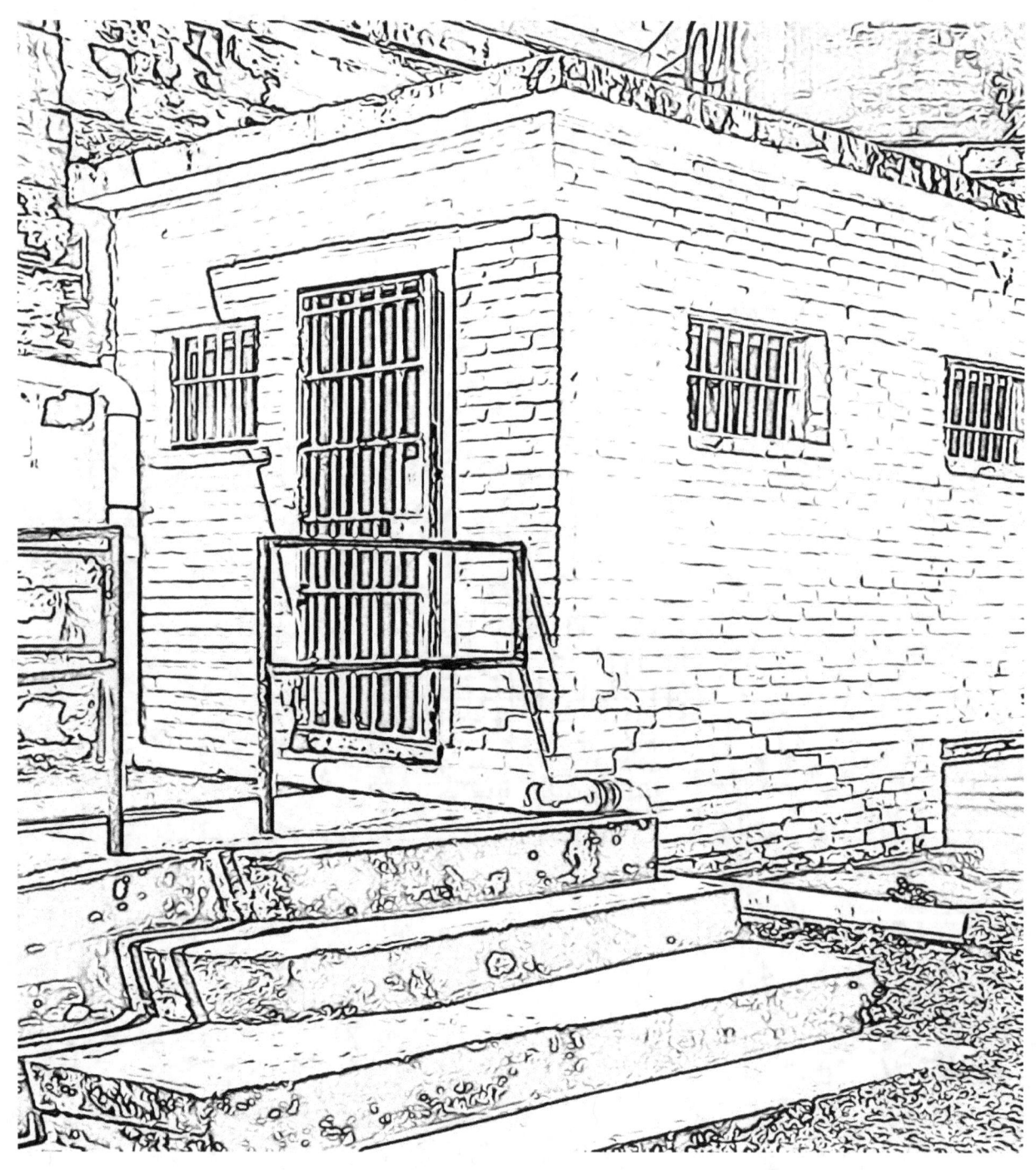

West Virginia Penitentiary

This was the Radio room in the South Yard. The name of the radio station was WPEN.

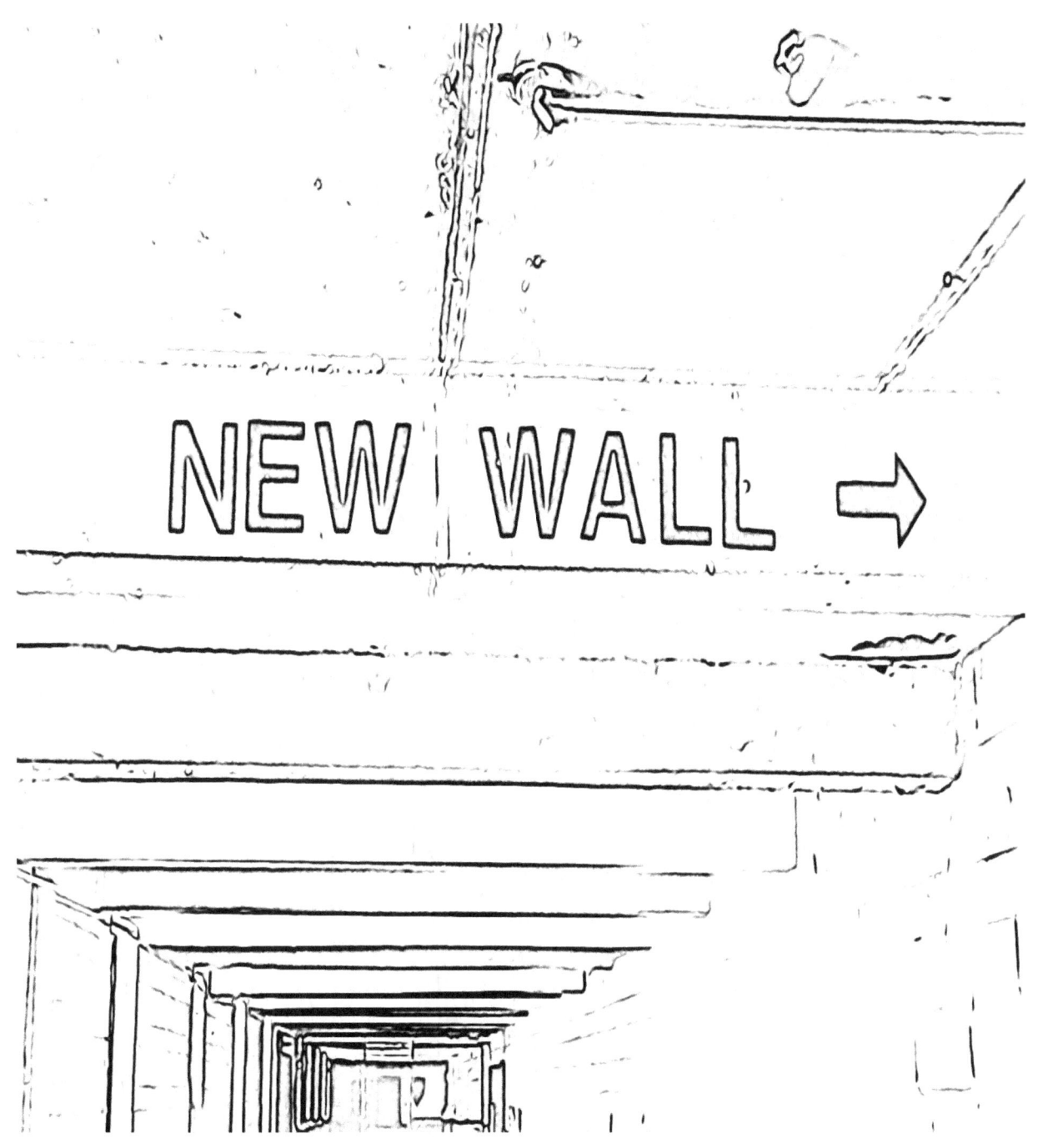

West Virginia Penitentiary

This is the 98 Corridor. This sign points to New Wall. New Wall has four sets of cell blocks – J, K, L, M.

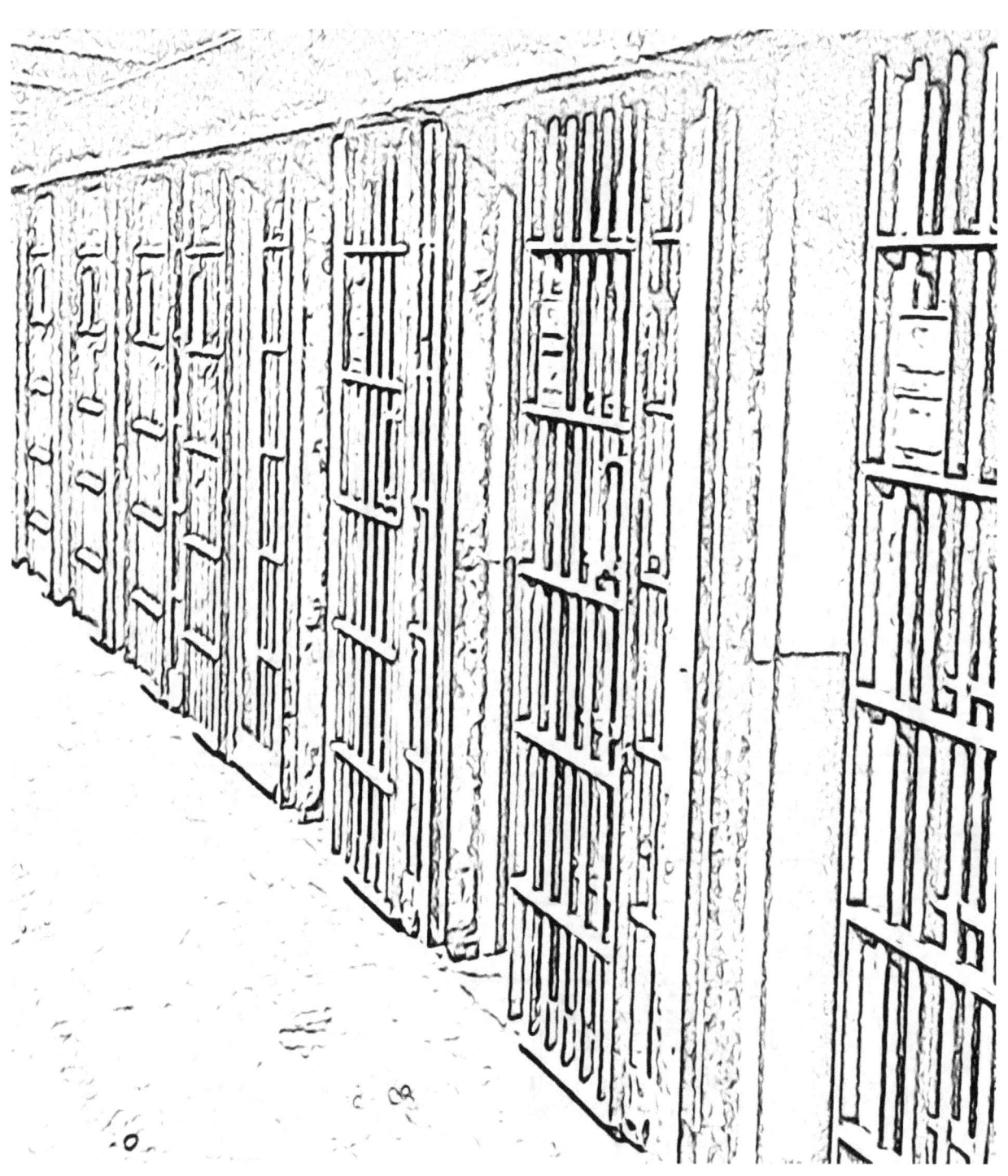

West Virginia Penitentiary

This is New Wall. These are cells in J Block.

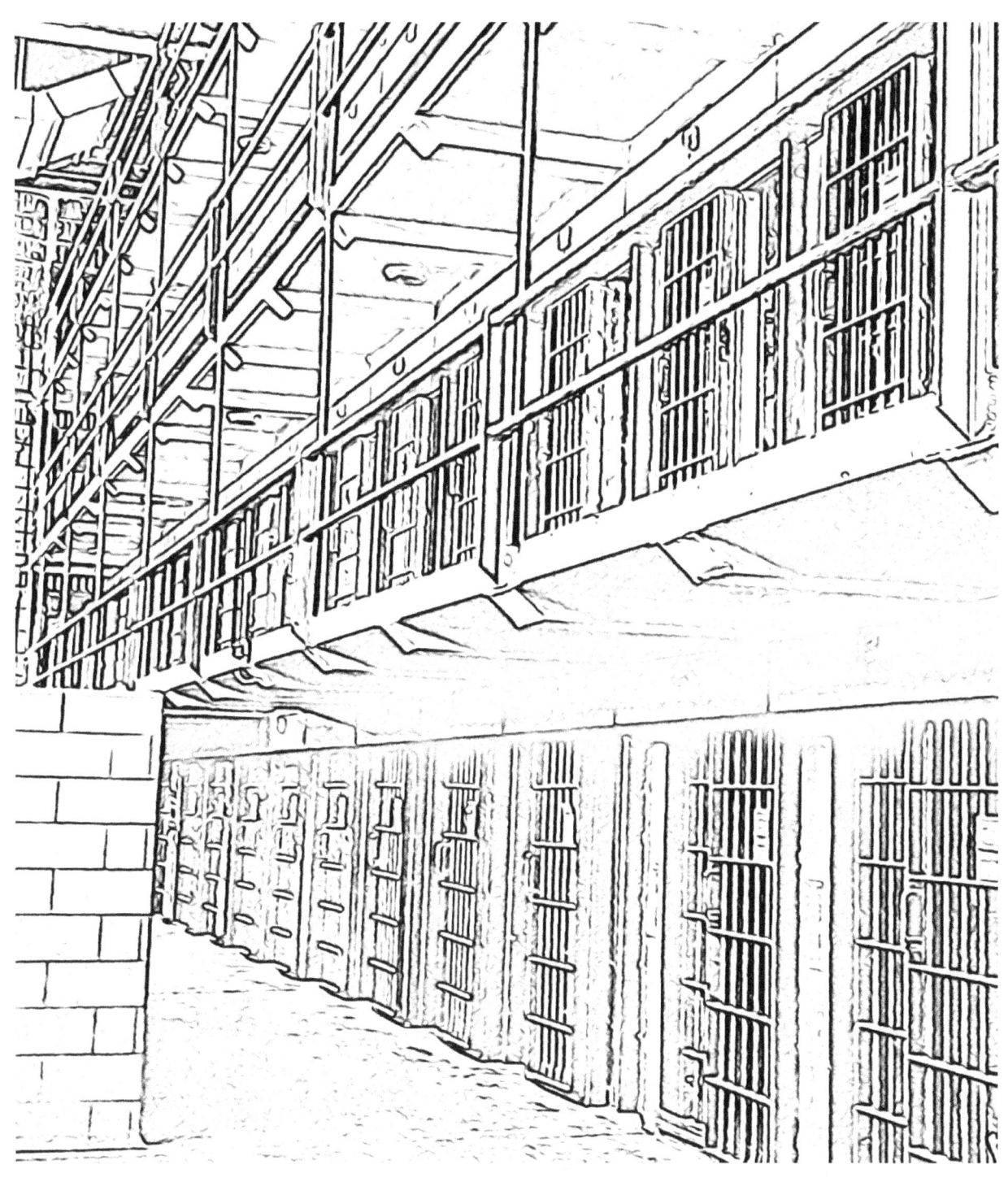

West Virginia Penitentiary

These are the tiers in J Block. Each cell block has four tiers.

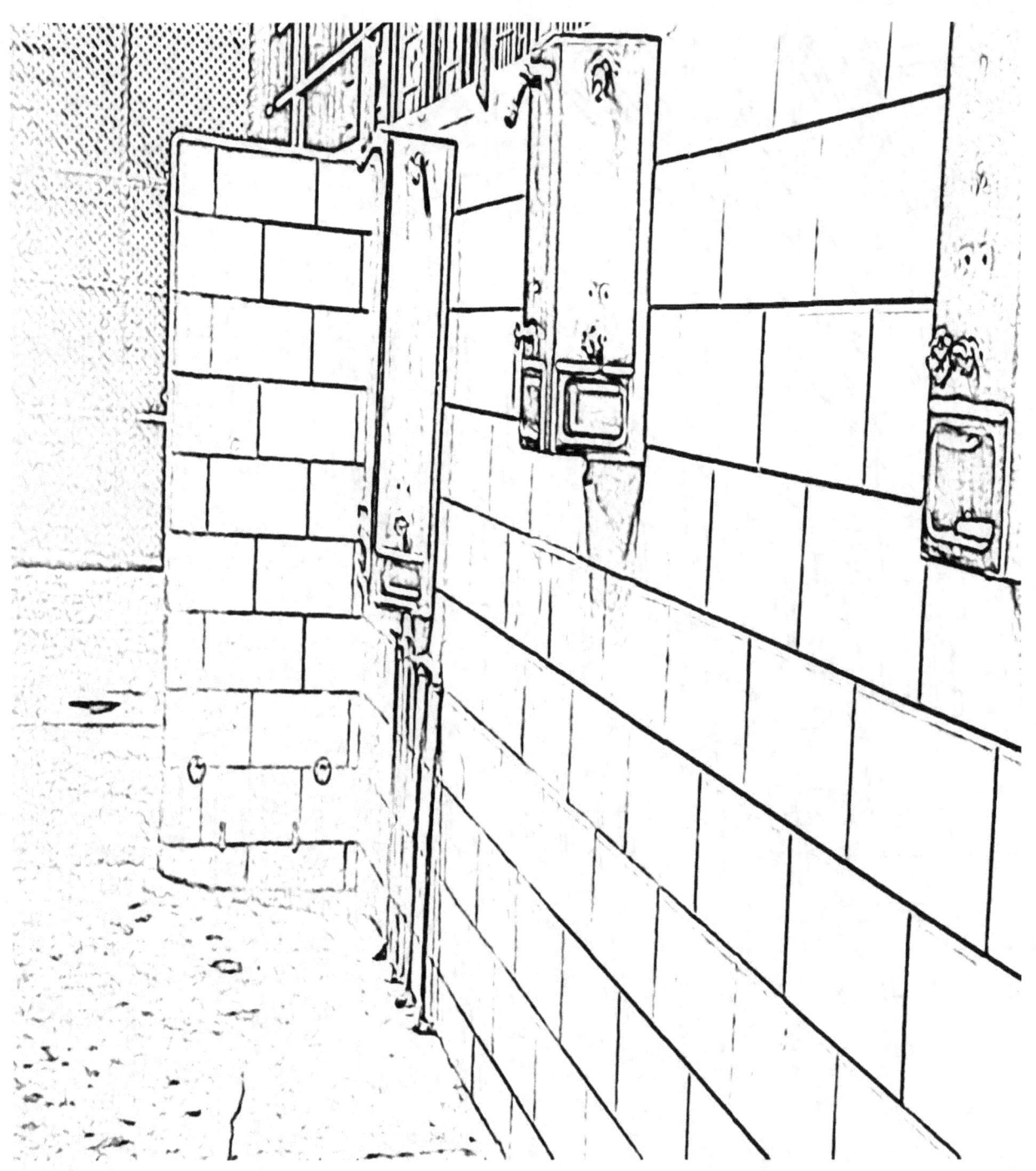

West Virginia Penitentiary

This is the shower area in J Block. Each cell block has its own shower area.

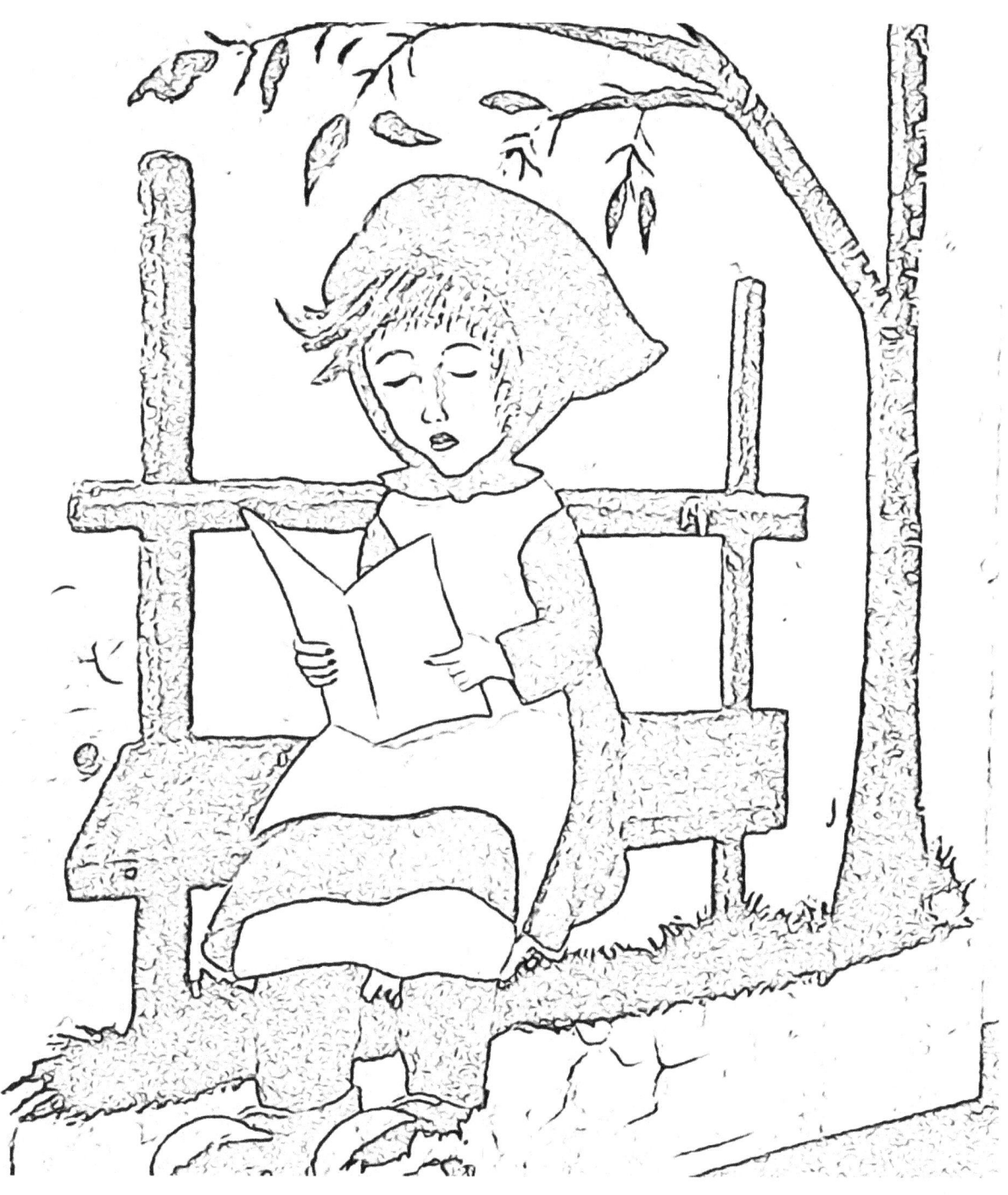

West Virginia Penitentiary

This is a picture on the wall by L Block. It was painted by one of the inmates.

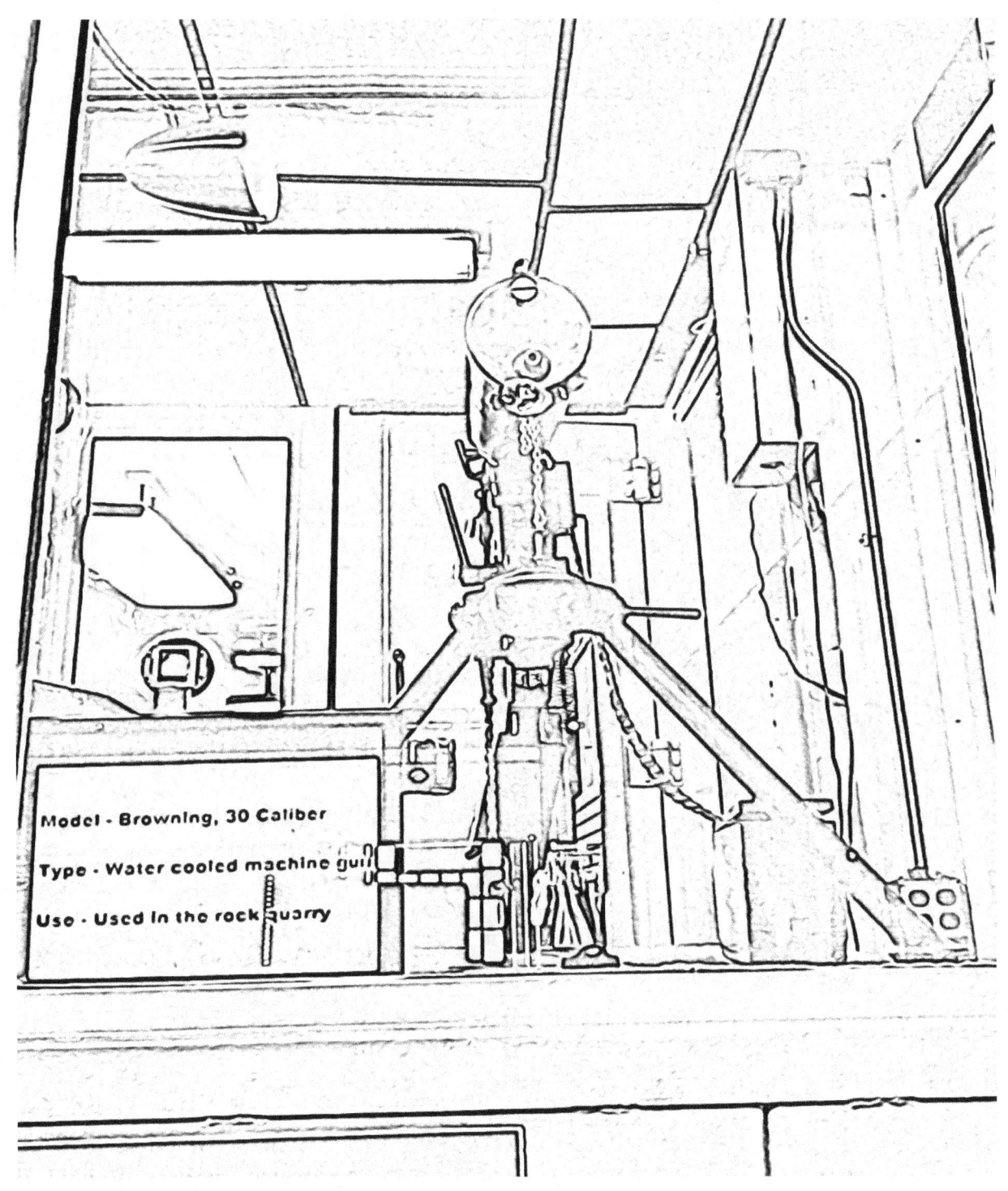

Model - Browning, 30 Caliber

Type - Water cooled machine gun

Use - Used in the rock quarry

West Virginia Penitentiary

After the tour, we see a machine gun that was used at our Stone Quarry.

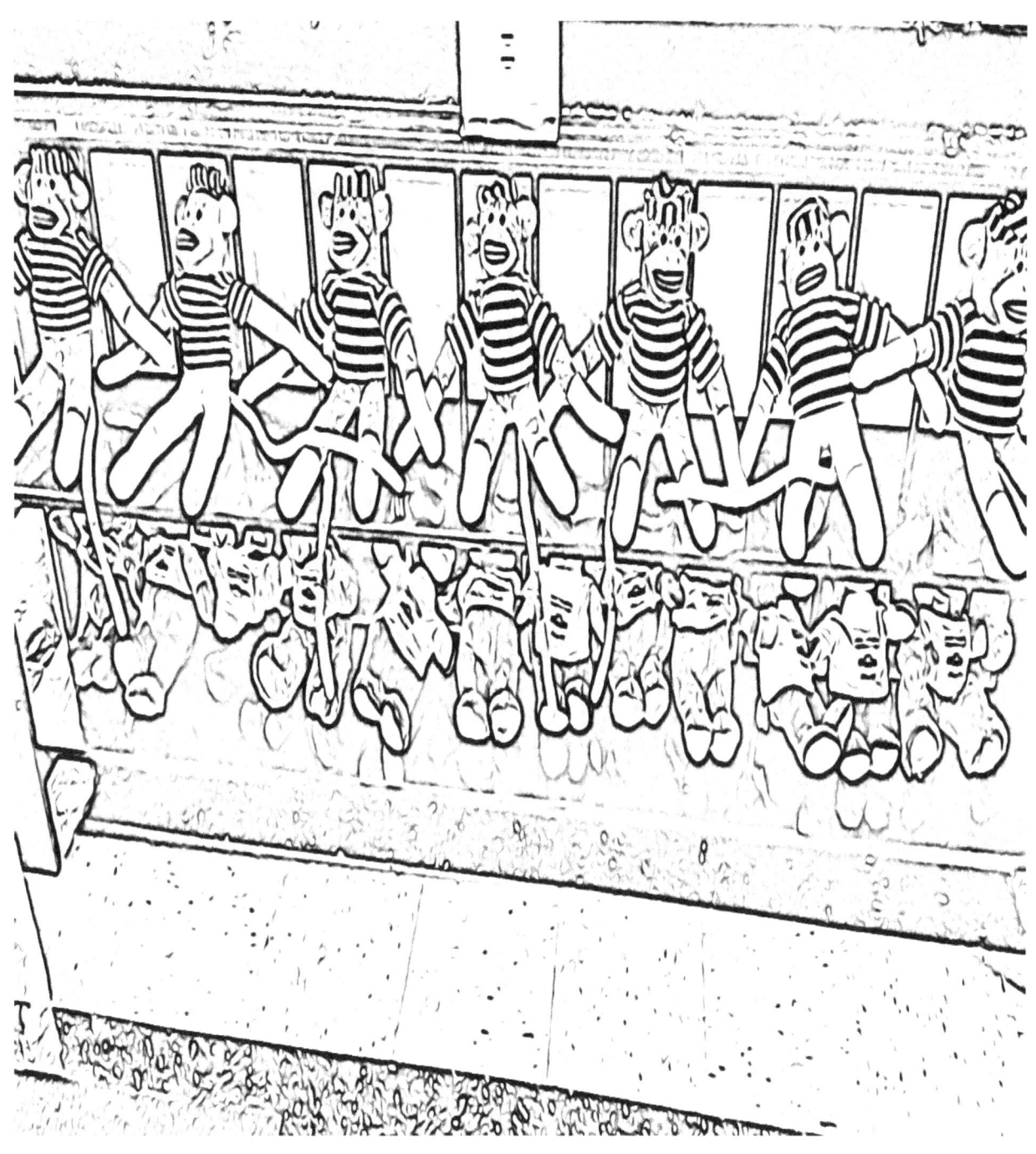

West Virginia Penitentiary

These are the only inmates left at the West Virginia Penitentiary.

COME
BACK
AND
SEE
US
AGAIN
AT
THE
WEST
VIRGINIA
PENITENTIARY!